My Life's

M000277877

TO: _____

The Lord has taken care of me by opening doors which enabled me to overcome many of the obstacles and hardships placed in my path that attempted to stop my progress during My Life journey.

Author: *Julius Green* Jr.

Julius Green, Jr.

Table of Contents

Dedication

This book is dedicated to my deceased parents, who provided for the family during the hard times on the farm in the 1930s and 1940s.

Acknowledgment

I would like to take this opportunity to say thanks to the following persons who were very helpful and patient with me as I put together the events, places, dates, times, and things. I will not forget the lessons that my father taught me about farming, including plowing and other tasks.

About The Author

I am a School License Marine Engineering Warrant Officer who served as a Chief Engineer onboard an Army Vessel at Fort Eustis, Virginia, and two tours in Vietnam.

I retired from the Army as a Deepsea Master Diver, having served at Fort Eustis, Virginia, Inchon Korea, Goose Bay, Labrador, and Sander-Strom, Greenland.

"Reflection on Years Gone By" is being published because I want future generations to see the struggles I encountered during my life journey.

This book will provide a brief history of how I have perceived the world in eighty-nine years of life. It is a look into my family history that hopefully will be cherished for many years in the future. If any portion of the book brings some joy or revelation to you, I will be thankful.

Foreword

This book is about a young Black man who grew up in the South in the township of Allendale, South Carolina. I attended school at Allendale County Colored Training School before segregation. On December 30, 1950, I voluntarily enlisted in the United States Army.

This is a compelling story about my trials and tribulation, the same probably experienced by many who grew up during segregation and were forced to excel and perform twice as better than white peers to break through social barriers and to satisfy family and parental expectations along with the inner self. As I am getting old, you know, many of my friends continue to ask me, why can't you sit down and write your life story to include your unique military experience, so the future generations will be able to see some of the hardships you encountered before and during segregation.

I had many thoughts about my memoirs, but who wants to read all of that stuff about someone. Furthermore, after you write all of that stuff and publish it, you have to find all your old friends, set up a table, put the book on display, and force your friends to buy one. No, I am not about to do that either.

These friends would let me off the hook for a year or two before the subject would come up again. So, I said to myself, maybe I need to tell my story while I can still think because time is running out. Well, before I start telling you my story, I should tell you a bit about where I grew up. It was a rural farming county, where the distance between family houses was about a quarter of a mile apart. There was no electricity, running water, bathrooms, force-air heating system, air-conditioners, etc. Instead, we had outhouse toilets with sears-roebuck catalogs for toilet paper, well-water, wood stoves and a chimney wood fireplace for heating and cooking, and kerosene lamps for lighting. When the sun used to set in the evening, if the moon and stars weren't shining brightly or there was a cloudy overcast at night, we were in total darkness until the sunrise.

In summary and reflection, little more needs to be said. My mother's love flowed from the mold of the family. My father and mother were God-fearing parents of compassion and understanding. Surely, Jesus has found a place for them at his Master's feet. So, to our parents, we love both of you, and we know that you are resting in peace.

Introduction

This book is dedicated with deep love, admiration, and appreciation, to the memory of our deceased parents Mr. Julius Green, Sr. & Mrs. Lizzie B. Green, both of whom contributed all that they had to our family, church, school, and community. To our cousin Maggie-May, who helped us better understand the real meaning of Christmas and the other holidays. To this union, they were blessed with three sons whose names were Warren, Willie, Julius Jr., and one daughter named Cornelia C. Green, all of whom resided in the home. I also had two half-brothers, James Green and Peter Doe. I was born in the County of Allendale, South Carolina, on January 24, 1932, in the home with the help of a midwife.

Chapter 1: 1932 Growing Up In Allendale, South Carolina

We lived on a farm approximately five miles from the town of Allendale in the country on Milton Place near Bostic Pond. It is where my parents were renting a two-horse farm on approximately fifty acres of land. We planted corn, cotton, peanuts, cucumber, watermelon, cantaloupe, sweet potato, white Idaho potato, butter beans, sweet peas, field peas, tomatoes, green peppers, red peppers, okra, green onions, garlic, sugar cane, rice, collard green, cabbage, string beans, squash, etc.

We attended school in the town of Allendale, South Carolina. At an African-American Segregated Allendale Country Training Colored School. We had to walk five miles each way, every day passing by a White School to get to our school. However, white students who lived in the county had school buses to ride to and from schools daily, and I want you to know that none of the buses were full.

The County School Systems

Allendale County had one white superintendent over thirty-four schools in the county and African-American students attended twenty-seven of these schools. We had three African-American principals in the three big schools. Each school had a number of classrooms with an office, libraries, dining halls, auditoriums, agriculture shop, music, and home economics. The names of these three schools were.

4

- Allendale Country Training Colored School
- Saint Marks Training School. (This one had an automotive training shop and screen-in outside building for teaching local farmer how to preserved food, such as canning using tin cans, and various sizes of mason jars.)
- Fairfax County Training School.

 A classroom teacher with a designated title of headmaster supervised twenty-four other schools. These schools were two rooms with a combination lounge room, with two teachers assigned to each school.

The total school population in the county was 3,950 students. Out of this number, 2905 were African Americans. The schools were operated by ninety-three teachers, with fifty-three of them being African-Americans. The per-capital teaching cost for whites was $73.56 and $4.58 for African-Americans. The total value for school property was $331.899 for whites and $41,570 for African-Americans.

Allendale County is served by Highway 301, 641, and 125. Two rivers form its boundaries, the Salkehatchie on the east, and the Savannah on the west, running through the center section of the county to the Choctawhatchee River.

5

The other little townships were Millville, Belloc, Martin, Appleton, Seagoville, Ulmer, Sycamore, Fairfax, Barton, Still-wood, and Ruddell.

Children Household Duties & Responsibilities

In our household, each child was assigned household tasks that were required to perform daily.

☐ To start the fire in the wood fireplace and the kitchen woodstove and ensure adequate wood and kerosene oil for lighting the kerosene oil lamps for illuminating the house each day.

☐ Ensure adequate amounts of wood and water are in the house daily for the wood fireplace and kitchen wood stove, and water for the family to drink and for bathing.

☐ Milk three cows and put them out to graze in the field, draw water from the well to make sure that an adequate amount of drinking water was available daily for the cows, mules, hogs, and to see that all of the animals were fed each evening during the week.

☐ My sister's duties were to make all beds in the house and help our mother with her daily tasks.

☐ Since we didn't keep the fire burning in the fireplace throughout the night in the winter, the temperature in the house would be virtually freezing at wake-up time, making it harder for anyone to get up from a warm bed with four layers of covering to start the fire. Once done, however, the fire maker became the most secure person in the household.

All of the above tasks had to be performed daily before we could get dressed for school. With a five-mile walk to and from school one-way, rain, shine, or snow, we had to be at school by 8.30 AM daily.

World War II

During World War II, there would be a black-out drill in the town of Allendale, and the emergency siren would sound off, and all of the lights in the town would be turned off. We were living out in the country and only had kerosene oil lamps for illumination. We would blow the flames in the lamps out and sit in the dark until the emergency siren was heard again to indicate that the town lights were turned back on. To me, it wasn't a drill. I thought that we were being bombed from the air. Once in a while, we would take the

7

mule and wagon to town to get various items, and while we were in town, we would see a hospital train passing slowly through the town, transporting hundreds of wounded soldiers. We could see the nurses and soldiers through the train windows. These soldiers showed signs of much suffering.

After The Depression

In 1938, a few years after the depression and several years before World II started, Allendale County's population was approximately 13,284. Of this number, 9,761 were African-Americans. Allendale was the county seat.

The Federal Social Welfare System was a much-needed resource for a large number of people in the region, primarily due to the lack of jobs. Social welfare assistance during the 1930s was provided to eligible families in the form of both cash payments and food subsidies. Like today, eligibility for assistance is based on family income and size.

Our family and others with similar borderline eligibility status were indirect recipients, getting food items from friends who received more food than they cared to use the items they didn't want. Oftentimes, children would help older recipients with the deliveries of their food items. In return, they would be rewarded with a small share of food items that included government surplus butter, American Cheese, raisins, dried apricots, canned peaches, whole wheat flour, canned meats, powdered milk and eggs, corn meal, dried pinto beans, and peanut butter. Some people would not have survived without food assistance during those depression years.

Race Relations

In most segregated Southern towns, race relationship has come a long way for the regions from the White Only and Colored Only signs in doctors' offices, hotels, motels, public restrooms, restaurants, train and bus stations. Signs were an explicit reminder that black African-Americans were relegated to second-class citizenship. Without the kindhearted white people and others like them, the road to national desegregation would have been continually filled with barriers. Occasionally, a segregated racial slur in the community would result in a fistfight among young people. Racial insults among adults were not uncommon, usually with the black African-Americans being on the receiving end.

In some cases, a fistfight resulted in the violation of the "peace code," and it was enough to cause the violator to spend at least a few days in the city jail. That was a situation, which was dreaded by most. Occasionally, you would hear the sound of the leather strap biting into a body, and piecing, screaming, and pleading for mercy was convincing enough for anyone passing by to fear going to jail.

Food Served In The Household Was Enjoyed

Like many mothers of the day, our mother operated the household on an extremely fixed budget. Yet on a (typical day, she demonstrated magic in providing three cooked meals for a family size seven for about seventy-five cents. Much of our food was homegrown and came directly out of our garden or our neighbors, in addition to green and yellow squash, vegetables, including rice, dried beans, Irish potatoes stew, fried chicken and other seafood stew, or soups. The gravy was made for many dishes to extend the quantity and add flavor, usually served over rice. The stew was made from chicken, pancreas, etc.

During the early 1940s, our family had several cows, which provided fresh milk with layers of cream that measured a half-inch on top of the milk bowl. We made butter and ice cream for the household. Sometimes, we would purchase commercial food items from one or two of the local country grocery stores. Our mother's shopping list was easy to remember. We only brought a ten-cent portion of coffee, sugar, dried beans, salt, black and red pepper, plus two loaves of fresh "light" bread. Those items would be supplemented with one or two freshly killed chickens from our yard or some salt meat from our smoke house, which were always available.

Given our mother's instinct for using herbs and other spices, we enjoyed her meals. She made Sunday meals

10

special with fried chicken or pot roast, homemade soup, green peas, potato salad complete with homemade mayonnaise, rising bread, sweet potato pie, or sweet potato bread and bread pudding. She also made ice tea, hand-crank cream, and cakes. All of her food was always tasty and delicious.

Early Drinking Water Source (Well) Water

During the early years in the thirties, whether you lived in the country or town, the source of water for drinking, watering farm animals, washing clothes, dishes, utensils, pots, pans, bathing, etc., was "well-water". The well-diggers would get together and build a square wooden box frame with four posts placed on all four corners of the wellhole. Two additional posts were made out of 6" by 6" wood, erecting these posts up across from post one on each side of the well frame. A piece of lumber would run across the top from post to post, with a swivel metal wheel attached to lumber in the center of the wellhole to be dug with a rope attached to five-gallon bucket used for drawing the dirt up and out of the hole while digging the well when digging was completed for pulling water from the well. Most wells were dug to a depth of 30 to 90 or more feet deep. However, if the well-digger finds a good stream of water at any depth, they stop there.

Once the well is completed, inspected and approved, by the county health department, we are ready to start watering our live stocks such as mules, cows, hogs' goats, chicken, birds, and for our family use.

Boy Cutting Lawn

Living in the country, we did not have to mow our yards because the grass was not allowed to grow in the yard, and if you did find grass in the yard, the first thing you would do is chop or hoe it up. The only thing that you would see in the yard would be beautiful flowerbeds. Yards were broom swept clean weekly or otherwise when our parents request that the lawn be cleaned. That meant sweeping.

Potbellied Stove

Coal was used for fuel in potbellied stoves and space heaters in school classrooms. It was the only source of fuel used in blacksmith shops due to its intensive heating capability to "soften" (make red hot) iron for it to be shaped into horseshoes, plowshares,

and other farm and commercial implements.

Some folks whose budget would allow used coal for fuel to heat their home. Those that had funds to spare would buy coals from a coal dealer. However, those who could not afford to purchase coal from a coal dealer, were allowed to go along the rail tracks to pick up the pieces of coal that had fallen to the ground off the filled gondola railcars.

Making And Flying Kites

Times were hard on the farm; during our upbringing as kids, we had to make all the things needed for self-entertainment, such as flying kites. We all looked forward to the month of March or a good windy day to fly our self-made kite. This was one of the most enjoyable pastimes. Kites were made in various shapes, sizes, in some cases colors, and for different purposes. The most talented folks used pictures of a kite and even life-sized self-portrait models. Practically all of the supplies needed to make a kite were available at home or at one of our playmate houses. Walter was my friend, who was thirteen years old, taught me the art of kite making. I was ten years old, and we made several models together before I branched out on my own. Making kites was as much fun as flying them. In my opinion, the kite described above was perhaps the simplest to make and was the most popular model during my teen year.

Boy Slapping Worn Tire

Another pastime sport was running behind, slapping used automobile tire. This was a fun thing to do for young boys and girls. Children would enjoy running behind "slapping" worn auto tires, keeping it rolling by hitting it with the open hand running up and down hills. Look like one on one ever got tired in those days.

Hog Killing Times

Several men in most communities were known to be skilled butchers, and their skills were in demand from approximately October until April annually. Each one of the butchers had a different flair, perhaps, but they were all experts at not only the slaughtering phases, but they could also cook crispy hog crackling, hog headcheese, and making link sausage and hog pudding. Our family raised lots of hogs each year on our county farm, and we usually scheduled the killing during the school fall break in October after the first frost fall so that it would not interfere with hog-killing time. My uncle Warren (Green) was our butcher, and my siblings and I were so excited being his helpers, almost all farmers within our community would help.

 The first order of business was getting the family large wash pot out and sit up on three to six bricks to get it about six to eight inches high above the ground then we would fill it with water and start a fire around the pot to heat the water until it boils in the wash pot, then we would put some red devil lye into the hot water.

The second order of business was to catch the hog to be killed and two men would hold the two hind legs of the hog, and someone would get a wood chopping ax and give a hard blow to the hog's head, knocking it unconscious and as the hog lay on the ground the butcher would use one of his sharp knives to stab the hog in its heart and allow its blood to spill onto the ground as the hog expired.

The third order of business would be to dig a slanted hole in the ground at a forty-five-degree angle then slide a fifty-five-gallon drum into the slanted hole in the ground and

16

return the sand dug from the hole back around the drum, then fill it with hot water from wash pot. Now drag the dead hog and put the head first into the drum, let it sit in hot water for about five minutes, then drag him out and reversed the hog position by sliding the rear end into the drum for another five minutes, then drag the hog out onto a flat board laying on the ground to remove all of the hair from the hog body.

The four order of business was to erect a number of poles with a cross 2" by 4'' inch piece of lumber nailed on to the top of the pole that is erected in a deep hole in the ground with braces on both sides to hold the weight of the hog. Then the butcher would cut two slits on each of the hog hind legs to find Grisel on each hind leg. Then two are three men would lift the hog up and hang it on the cross bars nailed to the upright pole, hanging hog with his head pointed to the ground.

The butcher would then make a precision cut to the hog's throat down to the neck bone. Then he wound start at the hog tail and cut along the hog's body straight down to its throat. Then he would remove the hog's internal organs (guts), separating the liver. The ladies would clean the guts and bury the waste in a deep hole that was dug in the ground. Some of the other ladies would take the hog liver, lights (lungs), and heart, remove all of the fat from around them and then wash everything clean. The body of the hog would be allowed to hang overnight to harden up so that the butcher would be able to dissect or cut it up into hams, shoulders, and milden off. After, separating the backbone from the neck bone, the butcher would then cut off all four feet from the hog. The feet would be cleaned, removing the huff, they would cut off the excess fat from the hams, shoulders, and milden, to include the inside of the hog. All of the excess fat parts were removed and cut into small pieces, then wash cleaned. Again, we would get out the big wash pot and start the fire completely around the pot to get it hot, and putting all of the fat pieces into the pot, letting these pieces cook into crispy crackling. We would separate the grease from the crackling by sifting it through a strainer, putting the grease into large containers. We would sprinkle a little salt over the crackling, let them cool, and then they were ready to eat or make a pan of crackling bread.

The hog hams, shoulders, milden, and the hog head (split in half) were salted downed, placed on the top of a cotton sheet, with the pine or wheat straw placed under. The meats were covered with straw on both sides of the meats on the floor area covered under a cotton sheet. All meats will stay in this position until the salt draws all of the water out of the meat. The meats would then be washed cleaned, making it

18

ready for the smoke house. Each piece of meat is hung from the ceiling in the smoke house. We would place hickory wood, pine cured bark and etc., to make a low smoke fire under the meat. We don't want a fire, just smoke sometimes, you have to wet the wood down where you get smoke only. The smoke will draw any remaining water from the meat and give it a hickory flavor. The meat was smoked for three to

four weeks. Then we would go into the smoke house and brush the meat down with honey to give it a blended flavor.

Living On A Farm

My family had a very productive farm crop in the year 1943, which gave my parents the opportunity, after paying off all their debts, with enough profit from their crop, to stop renting farm land from the Milton's, who were the land owners. In December 1943, just before the holiday season began, my parents had the opportunity to purchase their own farmland through a government program at that time. They were able to acquire one hundred and seventeen acres of farmland with approximately eighteen acres of timber with lots of pine, oak, and other types of trees.

We moved to our own farm, which came with a large farm barn or (building) with a loft on top with two covered wings attached on each side of the barn. One side was where a two-mule stable was located, with a stable gate to keep the mules in their stables. On the other side of the barn was where the hogs and cow pens had a gate with a fence attached to the other side of the barn with a large gate. Inside the fence, we had two water troughs. The long one was for the mules to drink from, and the other trough was for hogs to drink from. This farm came with a deep in-ground well for drinking water for the animals and the household. The large house had four large bedrooms, a living room with a built-in fireplace, a dining room, a large combination kitchen, and a lounge with a built-in fireplace. The family house came with a large front and back screened-in porch. The farm also had a large storage house for cotton etc., a smoke house with a covered shed on both sides. There was a chicken coop with built-in nests for the hens to lay their eggs. There was a big open yard with a fence and a gate for the chickens to exercise. The outhouse came with a built-in, dual side-by-side toilet seat. The only other thing needed to make the outhouse complete was Sears or Montgomery Ward Catalogs.

My parents farmed this land for a number of years, using one of two mules for tiling the soil and plowing. We had a yoke hookup for a one-mule plow and a two-mule plow. We planted corn, cotton, watermelons, cantaloupes, butter beans, sweet peas, cucumbers, peanuts, sweet potato, white Idaho potato, rice, wheat, rye, sugar cane, etc.

21

 Farming requires the farmers to plant each type of seed in rows with each row is separated about three to four feet between each type of seed is planted on his own acres of land, separate by plots. All of the other seeds will be planted the same way, with the exception of wheat and rye. These seeds will be broadcast continually in a field by the number of acres the farmer wants to plant. However, these seeds are planted in separate plots.

A typical farm day starts each day when the sun comes up, and my father would plow until 12:00 Noon. He would stop for one hour to feed the mule and himself. At 1:00 PM, he would start to plow again until the sun set. He plowed five days a week. If he did not accomplish enough work within those five days, he would plow on Saturdays until noon to get what he wanted to accomplish that week.

Please note that during months the sun does not get too hot on the farm during the day while on the farm. We had to get a certain amount of work done each day. In other words, the plants had to be plowed in order to produce a good harvest yearly. When plants like corn grew tall in its row, it was a cool and breezy wind when you were plowing. However, once you completed plowing the row to the end, you were exposed to the sun. You would not get any cool wind or a breeze until you got to the other end of the row. Before we moved to our own farm, we lived next to Bostic Pond, which was known for having a lot of large and small alligators. The alligators would sometimes migrate from one pond to another pond. While you were busy plowing, you could see the plants shaking from one side to the other in the row facing you. I would automatically know that an alligator was moving to another pond, and if he has his baby gators with him, you were in for a fight that day.

Mostly during the summer in July or August, we would pull leaves from the corn stocks and make them into small bundles together. The corn leaves were used to make fodder for the mules to eat. Once the fodder dries out, we would get the wagon and hitch up two mules to it, so we could haul the fodder from the cornfield along with the hay to the barn for storage in the loft. During the fall season, which was harvest time, the corn was taken from the field and put on the ground floor of the barn to be used to feed the hogs, cows, mules, and chickens, and the other farm animals.

We had a separate building for the cotton. When we picked the cotton, we stored it in the cotton house until we got enough to make a few bales. Then we would load the cotton into the wagon along with two or three sheets of cotton loaded on the top of the cotton in the wagon body. We would hitch two mules to the wagon to haul the cotton to the

Cotton Gin in town. Once we arrived at the Cotton Gin, we would get in the line and wait until our turn. The line moved extremely slow. When it finally got to be our turn, finally, we would move the wagon under the Gin's Suction Head. It would suck the cotton from the wagon to the Gin head, which would separate the cotton lint from the seeds and cotton. The cotton would go down one chute and seeds down another chute to the collection area. The cotton seeds would be weighed and sacked. The cotton lint would go to the bailer, which would bale the lint into five to six-hundred-pound bale.

One thing about living in the country and farming, all of the crops planted had to be completely harvested before the children could go to school. Sometimes we did not get to start school until late December or early January. It all depended on when all of the crops were completely harvested.

When we started harvesting our rice crop, we would cut the rice at the bottom of the stock, cut it into small bundles, tie each bundle together using swine string, and then stack each bundle in its upright position in the field to dry out. Once it is dried, we would put a certain amount of rice on a farm sheet, which is eight feet by ten feet square.

Then we would use a long wood pole to thrash the rice grains, sifting to separate rice grains from its husk. We would place rice grains into a cotton sack for storage in our farm barn. The husk from the rice would be scattered onto the field grounds to treat the soil.

During the start of harvesting our sugar cane crop, we would remove cane leaves from the cane stalks and then cut the cane stalk bottom. The stalks were placed in piles on the ground. After that, we would get our wagon and mule to haul the cane stalks to the cane mill. The stalks would run through a rotating press wheel, turning round and round on top of the rotating platform wheel. The wheel would squeeze the cane stalk until the cane juice came out of the stalks. The juice would empty into a large 55-gallon barrel. This press was sitting on a rotating platform with a long pulling pole that was being pulled by a mule walking around in a large circle to grind the cane juice out while leaving the mash.

Once the barrel was full of cane juice, everything stopped, and the barrel was emptied into a very large round pot inserted into a large brick platform with a chimney fireplace on one end. Once the fire in the fireplace started to heat up, the pot for cooking the cane juice into syrup was processed by someone straining the mash to separate the cooked syrup from the mash. The mash was put into a large 55-gallon barrel. Once the syrup was at the desired thickness, it would then be allowed to cool down. After this, the syrup was ready to be placed into one-gallon glass jugs, half-gallon, or quart jars to store the syrup until ready for use. The skim cane mash can be used to feed cows and hogs or used to make moonshine whiskey.

Move From The Farm To The City Of Allandale, South Carolina 1952

After Warren, Willie and I left home, and I volunteered for the United States Army on December 30, 1950. The only one left on the farm was my father to keep farming the land. He was then up in age at that time, with a declining health condition and a large farm to attend to. He was also somewhat short on funds to pay someone to help him on the farm. Therefore, the large white farmer whose land was adjacent to his land wanted to acquire this piece of land.

Somehow, the white farmer and the state government agents persuaded my father to sell him the farm land, which had one hundred and seventeen acres of tenable land, with seventeen acres of wooded land that had lots of pine trees that were ready to be cut down for lumber. My father could have sold the timber and made a lot of money from selling the trees and still sell the property to this farmer.

After selling the farm, my parents bought a large lot on 1½ acres of land with three bedrooms house which also had a kitchen, bathroom, large living room, long hallway, large back porch, and a front porch screened in that ran across the width of the house. The property also had a deep well for water and a storage house. This property was on the borderline of the city. At that time, sewage and city running water were not required. However, since that time, the city required all borderline property owners to hook into the city sanitation department for sewage and water.

The town of Allendale, South Carolina, back in the days when U.S. #301 ran from New York to Florida and through the center of my hometown, had a large train station with a depot for shipping farm goods by train. We also had five or six clothing stores, two drug stores, two hardware stores, two dry-cleaners, two cotton gin mills, a corn and grits mill, two large grocery stores, many little mom and pop stores, lots of service stations, two passenger trains - one coming from Columbia, South Carolina and the other from Augusta, Georgia. In addition, Allendale had cargo trains, a grey-hound/trail ways bus station, twenty-eight motels, two hotels, Kentucky Fried Chicken, several segregated restaurants for Caucasians and African Americans. Of course, this was during the days of Jim Crow. There were two automobile dealerships, a mechanic shop, Coca-Cola and Pepsi Cola plants, thirty-four schools, out of which twenty-seven were for African-Americans. However, the Causations students had buses to ride, while the African-American students had to walk to school.

When U.S. Highway #95 (US I-95) became a reality, all traffic going from New York to Florida now bypassed all of the small towns and caused the local motels, two hotels to close one by one. There were no motels or hotels within twenty miles from my hometown, and all bus and train stations, clothing and drug stores, dry-cleaners, the Coco-Cola and Pepsi cola plants, restaurants, corn, and grits mill, automobile dealerships, mechanic shops were closed. We now had three funeral homes left, two African-Americans and one Caucasian funeral home, two African-Americans and two Caucasian schools, and now that the schools are integrated, all students now have buses, the other twenty-four African-Americans were taught in two rooms schools that are now closed. My hometown now is considered to be a ghost town.

It just goes to show that over an extended period of time, and because businesses were built around Highway #95, the town of Allendale lost a lot of personal services. Today, when we go home, a lot of personal services, such as motels, hotels, restaurants, clothing, dry-cleaners, drug stores, etc., no longer exist because they went out of business.

Laundry Day

Every Friday was the traditional laundry day for most people throughout the region and beyond. Our mother used a number ten galvanized washtub for washing and another for rinsing. Washboards made of wood and corrugated tin or corrugated fiber glasses were used to scrub soiled cloths. With the help of warm water and an Octagon (home-made soap), the clothing items to be washed were submerged in the soapy worm water and repeatedly rubbed against the metal on the washboard in a downward and rotating motion until the item is "washed" clean.

The item was then twisted using both hands to "wring out" as much of the soapy water as possible before placing the items into the rinse water tub, heavily soiled clothes, such as our father's sometimes oily and grimy overalls and denim shirts resulting from his job, would be placed in boiling water using lye soap in a crackling pot over an open fire in the yard. The clothing would occasionally be stirred using a crackling paddle that resembled an oar.

After the washing and rinsing process and using clothespins, the clothes were hung on clotheslines made of galvanized wire that was stretched between two metal poles that stood about six to seven feet tall. Once the clothes were pinned onto the line, they were kept from touching the ground by using props. White clothing was done the same way, using modern bleach. This liquid concentrate, blue in color as the name implies, was used to "bring out" the whiteness.

Clothing or any household items that required ironing after drying were saturated in liquid starch solution in a small tub or basin and again, "wrong out" before being pinned to the clothesline. The liquid starch solution was prepared by combining water and Argo brand dry starch and cooking until the starch was dissolved. The "sprinkled" items would then be rolled separately and set aside for the dampness to penetrate the entire item. The clothing would then be ready for ironing, using a flat iron.

The Flit Spray Gun

Coping with roaches, chinches, and mosquitoes in the summer also brings a special challenge for anyone. For example, no matter how hard you worked at it. It is found that it is impossible to get completely rid of the roaches. These are large flying roaches that scattered and flew around the room whenever a light was switched on after being off for a while at night. Temporary control was about the best anyone could achieve.

In spite of screens, windows and doors, seemingly well-trained mosquitos would slip by flit insect spray to nip and hound you during the night. Chinches were a plentiful as the mosquitos.

These little bedbugs hid in crevices of the bedspring and mattress during daylight hours. But they came at nighttime for their ''meal.'' We used to sit on the side of the bed, pick them off the mattress, and squish them in old newspaper.

These bugs had a peculiar mall that resembled that of the pungent June bug. Although we haven't smelled a bedbug in over sixty-five or more years, I am sure I can immediately identify one by its smell.

The summer was also the season that moss-filled mattresses were ripped open, the moss aired or washed and dried or replaced with fresh moss collected by pickers from live oak trees. All m*attress ticking is washed during the summer and replaced an all beds in our home.*

The Outhouse

During the early years, outhouses played an obviously important role in family life. Looking back, it is a wonder that we were able to enjoy relatively good health. We did pay attention to possible contamination, however, by relocating the location of the outhouse annually. This required digging a new hole in another location approximately three feet wide, four feet long, and four or five deeps. Once dug, the old outhouse would be moved to

32

the new holes. Then you would move the dirt from the new hole dug to the old holes to cover it up.

It was a pleasure to do business in the new facility, which would be stocked with sale catalogs from Sears, Montgomery Ward, and discarded newspaper, made softer by crinkling the sheets together to soften the paper up to be used for toilet paper. Our family budget did not allow the toilet to be a priority in our household at the time. So, this was an accepted sewer system for the outhouse.

Taking Weekly Baths In Washtub

A simple chore like taking a bath required extra effort and cooperation from family members to help fill and empty the washtub. During the summer months, the temperature of the running water in the cistern stream was ideal for bathing. During the winter, water was heated on the kitchen wood stove. Since the kitchen was the warmest place in the house, bathing was more comfortable there. A few of us didn't seem to mind bathing after someone else, using the same water. It was a resourceful (and convenient) thing to do.

My family budget would not allow us to live high on the hog. However, later on, some family's budget allowed them to purchase portable kerosene heaters. The bathroom was eventually used for baths during the cold months. The addition of the kerosene cooking stove followed later.

Wood Cutting: An "Industry"

During the early year's woodcutting was respected as another skill required to develop a needed household product used to fuel cooking all year-round and fireplaces during the winter. Woodcutters often used a block of wood to chop it into desired chuck size with an ax and stack it in half-cord (four feet long and four feet high), and a full cord measured if stacks were to be sold or stacked in any fashion when the wood was for home use. The stacking allowed the sun and the air to dry the wood cut from "green" or uncured logs to facilitate burning.

Our family normally would go into the woods and select certain green trees to cut down or trees already on the ground, to cut up into fire length wood for the fireplace, and certain smaller size wood length for the stove. During the summer months, we would cut enough wood to last us through the winter months. Then we would load the wood into our wagon, using mules to pull the wagon to our house, and place it in our woodyard. We would then separate the wood into fireplace length and the smaller pieces for the cooking stove wood.

We also would go into the woods to look for pine stomps that were vetted with pine tar. Once we located that stomp, we would dig it up and cut it into pine splinters that were used to start the early morning fire daily or whenever the need arose to make a fire.

Chapter 2: Volunteer For United States Army

I stayed on the farm plowing and during various other things that needed to be done on the farm until I finish the tenth grade in high school. During the summer of 1950, I asked my parents to let me go to Jacksonville, Florida, to stay with a cousin who owned the Richmond Hotel located at 422 Broad Street. I was to stay there until the end of the year. However, during that time, I would work helping out at the hotel on shifts. Sometimes at days and other times night. So, I made an arrangement with my cousin that during my spare time I could get a part-time job and still help her at nights and all day on weekends.

I was able to get a job working at a service station pumping gas, etc. The Richmond Hotel had a contract with the Armed Forces Recruiting Station that was located in the United States Post Office downtown Jacksonville to house young African-American Military Recruits. These recruits had to have passed their aptitude tests for entry into their respective branch of service.

The recruiters would come to the hotel on various occasions to check on various recruits to tell them what camp or fort that they would be shipped to for their basic training. So, one day I happened to be in the hotel when one of the recruiters came in and saw me. He immediately asked me would I like to enlist in the service, and I said yes. The recruiter then said, "If you pass the aptitude test, you will be eligible for enlistment into the service." The rest is history.

My group of African-American recruits was shipped from Jacksonville, Florida on the night of December 30, 1950, in a segregated sleeper rail car. The white recruits were in the same type of car with the destination set to Columbia, South Carolina for basic training at Fort Jackson. We found the post to be totally integrated.

Upon our arrival at the train depot in Columbia, South Carolina, the Army had buses waiting for the train. A big bad Noncommissioned Officer (NCO) Sergeant was sent to welcome and transport all U.S. Army new recruits to the base. All recruits, African-American and white, heard the loud barking orders coming from the big bad Sergeant stating, "Get your asses off this got dam train and onto those buses outside so that they can transport your asses to Fort Jackson, South Carolina for processing into the got dam army."

After all the recruits were processed, we were given the necessary clothing and then marched up to tank hill for assignment to the cadre battalion, who had all of the basic training instructors. They were responsible for conducting all elements of basic and advanced infantry training. The battalion personnel officers first assigned all the white recruits to various Companies, A-H, within the battalion. Then, the battalion personnel officers would divide the African American recruits into an equal number and assign them to Companies A-H. This method ensured that the white soldiers always outnumbered the African American soldiers within each Company.

The training battalion had all basic companies start their infantry basic training during January 1951 for a period of eight weeks that included rifle training. There, you had to learn how to field strip and cleaned all parts of the weapons, including disassembling and reassembling your rifles, M-1 pistols, machine guns, and bazookas. After all of the above was done, you were considered ready to go to the rifle range. There, you were required to qualify for each one of these weapons by earning a passing score. Next, you would march to the field or woods to learn how to dig one and two-man foxholes, pitch a two-man tent to sleep in each night while you were in the field.

Next, you would be required to go on long marches, walking with all of your assigned equipment in your backpack strap to your back. Your training cadre would march you until he was ready to return back to your company area. Each morning at about 5:00 A.M., the training cadre would come into the barracks and turn on the overhead lights, yelling, "Get up." Reveille would be 45 minutes, starting at 5:45 A.M. During that time-line, you were expected to make up your bunk, do your personal hygiene, and be fully dressed in uniform, making sure that you had everything in order and be in formation when reveille was called.

The First Sergeant would call the roll. When your name was called, you would answer, "Yes, Sergeant!" At the end of roll call, anyone who had not answered would be counted as not present, would be considered (AWOL) absent without leave. The First Sergeant would dismiss the formation, and everyone would fall out to the mess hall for breakfast and be back in formation by 7:00 A.M. to start Physical Training (PT). Strenuous exercises, such as Push-ups, Pull-ups, Sit-ups, jogging in place, Straddle horse, hop skips and jumps would be performed. We would be asked to lie flat on the ground, on our back with our legs in the air, opening them wide and then closing them several times. There were many other grueling exercises.

Once Physical Training (PT) was done, we would then get back in formation and the cadre would be there to pick up the troops at 8:00 A.M. for us to reassemble in formation to start daily training.

Our graduation ceremony was in late May 1951; therefore, all basic trainees was given orders for thirty days leave or (vacation) to travel to their various home states, and local townships or counties for recreation and relaxation before being shipped to Camp Kilmer, New Jersey. Camp Kilmer was the Port of Debarkation for processing all soldiers being shipped to the European Theater. The USS Sturgeon was a Troop-Ship, an Ocean liner, which transported approximately three thousand troops for the Port of Embarkation in Bremerhaven, Germany. There, we would wait for further assignments. The trip took twelve long days.

ASSIGNMENT TO GERMANY

From there, several of us were given orders to travel to various stations in Germany and assigned to a segregated African American Battalion located in Willesden, West Germany. There, I was assigned to the 373rd Armored Infantry Constabulary Company. I served there until our battalion and Company was deactivated. From there, our Battalion Personnel officer was given orders to send five black soldiers to integrate each one of the white companies throughout Europe. The orders were to ensure that the U. S. Army in Europe was totally integrated by the April 1952 directives.

From Wildflecken, Germany, I was given orders to travel to the 18th Infantry Regiment located in Aschaffenburg, Germany. I was assigned to Company C of the 18th Infantry regiment. When the First Sergeant and the Company Commander got the directives that his unit was getting four black soldiers and one a blackbuck (Enlisted Rank E-5) Sergeant, the Captain told the first Sergeant, that when we arrived, he was to make sure that I the buck Sergeant, came directly to see him.

Upon our arrival to the unit, the First Sergeant told me that the Commander needed to see me once I put all of my equipment in my assigned place in my platoon barrack. So as soon as I got my things in place, I reported to the Commander. The first thing that he wanted me to know was that the Army sent us to his unit, but they (He and his Unit) were not ready for integration. Additionally, I was going to have a racial problem with some of the white soldiers in his Company, he said. I immediately asked him what type of problems was he was talking about? He told me that his unit had soldiers from all over the racial South and various other places. They were not yet ready to take orders from a black squad leader with the rank of a buck Sergeant. He went on to say that he is required to assign me as a squad leader in a platoon. I told the captain that it was my understanding that the Army Regulations states that rank has its privileges in the Army. With me being a Black African American Buck

Sergeant squad leader in his unit, the only racial problem I saw was those white soldiers to be assigned to my squad. I told him they are the ones who will have a racial problem.

I also told him that the thing I am asking is for him to back me up when I take dispensary action against anyone of the members of my squad. The captain said to me, "Well, looks like you can handle it. What do you want me to do?" I said, "Give me those soldiers that you plan to assign to my squad, and I will interview them to see if any of them have a problem taking orders from me, an African American as their squad leader. The one that would have a problem, I would send that soldier back to you, and you are to send a replacement."

Not any one of the soldiers I interviewed had a racial problem with me. I served in this company until December 1953, and there I was given orders to return to the United States at Fort Jackson, South Carolina.

At Fort Jackson, South Carolina, I could always do things during my off-duty time on the weekends. Therefore, I had the opportunity to check out some of my old girlfriends I had known before joining the Army. They lived in my hometown, which was only seventy-nine miles from Columbia and Fort Jackson, South Carolina. Since the base wasn't very far away, when I had time off on the weekends and sometimes during weekdays, I would visit my

hometown. That gave me plenty of time to get into trouble and whatnot.

To my surprise, some of these old girlfriends had gotten married and had one or two kids. The others had migrated to other places and were heavily involved in some other type of relationship. All of them seemed to have a different outlook for their future than mine. However, while I was in Germany, my sister and my mother had selected a beautiful and attractive young lady for me to meet because they thought that she would be a good match for me as a wife.

I was introduced to her when I returned home. At first, I paid no attention to her, but as time went by, I had a lot of time to look over my life, consider my future and my direction. I began thinking to myself, "Boy, you better wake up, slow down and take a look at that attractive young lady that's been hand-picked for you."

She had a college degree, was employed in the local school systems, and came from a religious family. A sheltered young lady who was looking to have a great future with someone that God would send to her as a good soul mate.

44

As time went by, I had time to look at our relationship and think things over about our future. I found myself thinking that it was time for me to go back and take another look at this young lady. After we courted each other and talked about what each of us wanted out of life, that was the moment we decided that we would see what was in the future for us.

After that moment, the rest was history. We dated for over a year before we decided to get engaged. On August 7, 1955, Mrs. Lottie Cave Green became my wife.

After we were married and our honeymoon was over, she moved to Columbia, South Carolina, so we could be together. We rented a room and shared a kitchen and bathroom with the homeowner. We went on to live together as husband and wife for twenty-eight years until one night she went to play bingo in the February of 1983. It was a game that she loved to play during her off time from school or if she was not participating in some of her other organizations, such as her sorority, or shrine daughters of Isis, etc.

That night she had finished playing bingo and was leaving the bingo hall on her way home. Just as she was exiting the bingo hall, she passed out, fell on the ground with a massive heart attack. I got a call around 10:00 P.M. that night from her girlfriend saying come, and come at once. About ten inches of snow stood on the ground, and her girlfriend would not tell me what was wrong. So, I got our other car out of the garage, and I drove to the bingo hall.

As I was approaching the hall, I could see the rescue Para-Medics vehicle, along with the fire truck with their red lights on. As I approached the Para-Medic's vehicle, I could see one of the medics talking to the emergency room doctor in Mary Immaculate Hospital. I asked the medic how my wife was doing, and the only thing he said was, "Your wife is a sick person." I moved her car closer to the bingo hall and left it there overnight.

While moving the car, I noticed that the rescue vehicle had taken off enroute to the hospital. I asked one of the Fire Captains where they were going. He said, "To the emergency room." The doctor told them to take her to Mary Immaculate Hospital. I went there and signed her in.

I waited in the waiting area for a while. No one came out to tell me how she was doing, so I went to the front desk to ask the receptionist where my wife was located. She went to see the doctor in the emergency room, and he sent his nurse out to tell me that he was working on her and he would come out and explain her situation to me. The doctor came out and said, "Your wife has expired." I told the doctor that I would have an autopsy done before I called the funeral home.

The doctor told me that the pathologist would be at the hospital the next morning around 10:00 A.M., so I should first meet with them. They could tell me what time her body would be ready for pickup by the funeral home. I had a wake service and funeral for her in Virginia before I had her body transported to Norfolk Airport for air transportation to Columbia, South Carolina. Cave Funeral Home of Allendale transported her body from Columbia back home to Allendale, South Carolina. We had another wake and funeral at Union United Methodist Church with Interment in the family cemetery in Kline, South Carolina.

UNITED STATES ARMY DIVING SCHOOL;
FIRST U.S. ARMY AFRICAN AMERICAN DIVING OFFICER;
SECOND U.S. ARMY ENLISTED MASTER DIVER

DIVING COURSE
TRANSPORTATION SCHOOL MOS 564, 20 CLASS 9
FORT EUSTIS, VA. JAN 1956

When I applied to attend the U. S. Army Diving School, the first requirement was that each candidate meet all of the qualifications in compliance with AR 611-75, which required that anyone applying for divers training must have a physical examination at his local post. Upon the local doctor's approval, this physical must be sent to U.S. Army Surgeon General in Washington, D.C., for final approval.

The Army Regulation AR 611-75 stated that divers must be in grade E-6. So, when my physical was returned from the Surgeon General, stating that I was approved to attend the U. S. Army diving school, I was given orders. Thus, I was transferred from Fort Jackson, South Carolina to Fort Eustis, Virginia to attend the U.S. Army diving school.

However, upon my arrival, I was told that the diver course had already started and the next class would start in January 1956. I was mil-assigned to the 48th Transportation Truck Group, due to my MOS being excess to the post.

I was given orders from the 48th Transportation Truck Group to attend the diving school in late December 1955 to attend the diving class starting in January 1956. Upon my arrival at the diving school, the first thing I noticed was there were ten students in the class who were in pay grades E-3, E-4, E-5, and one additional in pay grade E-6. The first thing that came to me was that if you were an African-American candidate, you had to be in pay grade E-6. The Caucasians, on the other hand, were allowed to enter diver school at any pay grade.

Our diver class started with the diver's recompression chamber, which gives the school instructors the ability to test each student at various pressures depths to see that they meet all of the requirements to become an Army Salvage Diver. After passing the pressure depth test, we started classes in basic diver academic training in classrooms setting.

All diving students were trained on various types of rope sizes, strength, and how to make various knots, including splicing and tying various size ropes together surface and underwater. Divers were trained on how to identify and make repairs on all of the diver's equipment such as divers' dresses, mask, helmet, belts, shoes, lines (air-hose), telephone reset cable, air-compressors and different kinds of compressors, shallow-water equipment (jack-brown), such as suits (dress), mask, belt, shoes, hoses and all associated equipment, scuba tanks, mask, fins, dress, belts.

Each diver had to know how to assemble and disassemble all diving equipment dress underwater with a diver's tender to give various signals and directions. These included directions such as whether the diver needs to go right, left, forward, backward, take up or give slack in his air-line (hose), come up to the first decompression stop, or to the surface. If the diver asked his tender for a tool, rope, or whatever he needs, the tender would send it to him so he can get his job or project done promptly. The tender and diver had to know everything associated with diving.

TYPES OF ARMY DIVERS CLASSIFICATIONS AND PAY PER-MONTH

- ☐ 2nd Class $150.00
- ☐ Scuba Diver $165.00
- ☐ Salvage Diver $175.00
- ☐ 1st Class Diver $215.00
- ☐ Master Diver $340.00
- ☐ Diving Officer $240.00

Deep-Sea Diving Outfit

- ☐ Diving Helmet was 54 Lbs.
- ☐ Diving Shoes with lead soles was 40 Lbs.
- ☐ Diving Rubber suit was 18 Lbs.
- ☐ Diving Belt leather with lead weights was 84 Lbs.
- ☐ Diving Knife with brass shield was 7 Lbs.
- ☐ Divers Tool bag was 7 Lbs.

Total Gross Weight 210 Lbs.

Shallow Water Diving Outfit

- ☐ Jack brown mask with diving air hose
- ☐ Jack brown diving rubber suite
- ☐ Diving belt leather with lead weight
- ☐ Diving tool bag

Self-Contained Underwater Breathing Apparatus

- ☐ Scuba Diving Regulator with face mask

- [ ] Scuba Divers' Twin Tanks charge with air
- [ ] Scuba Divers' canvas belt with lead weight
- [ ] Scuba Divers' rubberize Suite
- [ ] Scuba underwater waterproof light
- [ ] Scuba Divers' Knife, etc.
- [ ] Scuba Divers' Underwater Camera

U.S. Army divers were trained in the following specialties

- [ ] Underwater Salvage Operation
- [ ] Surface Salvage Operation
- [ ] Surface and underwater demolition
- [ ] Surface and underwater welding, cutting and burning
- [ ] Arc-Art Welding, cutting and burning using this (air)
- [ ] Underwater surveying the bottom of ships, etc.
- [ ] Underwater jetting and excavating of soil

Installing underwater brace on piers, etc.

- [ ] Using pneumatic saw to cut underwater piling in shallow and deep water
- [ ] Building surface piers in shallow or deep water
- [ ] Service and repairing underwater gas pipelines in shallow water or deep water
- [ ] Cleaning sea strainers and removing rope and cable from the ship's propeller blades.
- [ ] Using water to jet piling in the ground as needed

- Operating a diving barge using two sea mules to move the diving platform to and from diving sites where diving operations being conducted
- Operation of a dive decompression chambers to treat divers as needed during emergency situations.
- Operating various types of diver compressors to include limited maintenance

Basic diver training was conducted in the dive tank adjacent to the building (2716), which was thirty-three (33) feet round and thirty (33) three feet deep in all aspects of deep-sea, shallow-water, scuba diving in surface and underwater training. In addition, the following underwater diving training on how to perform various projects that conducted in the dive tank had to be demonstrated:

- Each diver must demonstrate his ability to dress and undress the diver and tend him while he is in the water.
- Each diver must demonstrate his ability in breathing while descending to the tank bottom area and how to ascend back to the top surface.
- Each diver must demonstrate his ability on how to use various types of tools in performing various projects on the surface and underwater.
- Each diver must demonstrate his ability on how to use pneumatic air tools at various depths underwater.

☐ Each diver must demonstrate his ability to use various types of demolition explosives on the surface and underwater in a safe manner.

☐ Each diver must demonstrate his ability to use a galvanometer for checking out the electric circuit to see that the system is open.

☐ Each diver must demonstrate his ability in using electric blasting caps and primer cords used while setting up an explosive in a safe manner.

☐ Each diver must demonstrate his ability on the use of an electric blasting machine, how to use to ignite explosives, etc.

☐ Each diver must demonstrate his ability to assemble a one-or two-man square pipe flange together underwater in the tank and in the 3rd port James River while dealing with the heavy deep mud on the bottom at various water depths.

☐ Each diver must demonstrate his ability to performed underwater welding, cutting and burning, on the surface and underwater with proper penetration in each bead.

☐ Each diver must demonstrate his ability to perform Arc-Art welding in cutting, using air to blow out the meld silage during cutting arc burning.

☐ Each diver must demonstrate his ability to perform underwater surveying instruments to determine underwater area conditions.

53

☐ Each diver must demonstrate his ability to perform surveys of the underwater hull of army ships. He must check the sea-strainers and if the strainers were clogged, he was required to remove any debris that may have caused the engines to run hot and make all necessary repairs as needed. In addition, he was required to prepare written reports on his recommendations to the ship's Captain of the underwater hull's conditions.

☐ Each diver must demonstrate his ability to perform underwater jetting to clear out debris on the channel bottom area and to excavate loss soil to the surface or unto a floating barge.

☐ Each diver must demonstrate his ability to perform repairs on wooden piers, piling, decks, and installed underwater bracings to stabilize or strengthen the overall piers condition. He can also jettison piling in the ground to replaced damage piling on piers and etc.

☐ Each diver must demonstrate his ability to use all types of underwater pneumatic saws use in cutting various objects such as falling trees, underwater stumps that are blocking underwater channels used to get ships or boats in and out of a pacific area.

☐ Each diver must demonstrate their ability to work as a team using a two-man crosscut saw to manually cut logs, or piling on the surface and underwater. Each diver is to make sure that his air-hose line is clear of being cut while they are performing the task.

☐ Each diver must demonstrate their ability to work as a team to construct a pier as per request in shallow or deep water to aid the requestor in any and all mission requirements.

☐ Each diver must demonstrate his ability to make various repairs to an underwater fuel pipeline that is six-inch, eight-inch or twelve-inch that runs miles out in the sea where large super-tankers cannot sail into waters less than fifty feet deep.

☐ Each diver must demonstrate his ability to fabricated a one-man wooden box in various depths underwater by nailing the pieces together, starting with the end pieces then the side pieces and while during so, he is to make that not one piece of board float to the surface, when that happen your project is rated incomplete. Therefore, the diver had to start all over.

☐ Divers are trained to work as a team on projects. They are to demonstrate their ability to fabricate a two-man wooden box at various depths underwater. Once both divers arrive at the bottom, they would check out everything needed to build the two-man wooden box. This requires that each diver would take an end pierce out of the project bag and make adjustments where one of the divers would pull a piece of lumber out of the bag and hand one side to the other diver. Then both divers would nail his side to the end piece he's holding, then pull another piece of lumber and nailing the same until the wooden box is completed and float to the surface. There, the instructors would grade the diver team on their efforts, good or bad.

☐ The need for steel cluster-pilings in the length of one hundred and fifty (150') feet long to be placed in groups of six pilings per cluster group and three groups of cluster piling needed to tie up a T-5 tanker ship as it discharged the fuel through the steel pipelines that transferred the fuel from the tanker ship to the tank farm that was located some five miles away.

☐ The diving instructors are to ensure that they meet all of the requirements to become a salvage diver, tested on each of the above tasks.

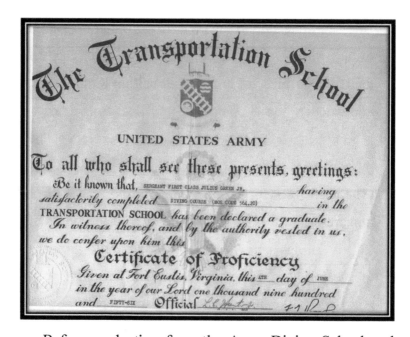

Before graduating from the Army Diving School and unbeknownst to me at the time, the senior diver assigned to the 73rd Transportation Company told the Company Commander that an African-American diver was graduating from the diving school. He also said that it is possible that he would be assigned to the 110th Transportation Battalion for further assignment to the 73rd Transportation Heavy Boat Company. He cautioned that my Caucasian divers would not take orders from me.

The company commander was convinced that the Caucasian divers would become problematic with my assignment, so he immediately addressed my assignment to the battalion commander. The battalion commander went to the group commander. They all agreed that I should be given an assignment in my old Military Occupation Specialty (MOS) rather than be assigned as a U.S. Army Salvage Diver in the 73rd Transportation Heavy Boat Company. And so, a call was made to the Post Personnel requesting that I, the U.S. Military's Second Enlisted African-American Diver, be given orders for assignment in his old MOS because there were no diver positions in the group for him.

MY REALITY UPON GRADUATING FROM THE DIVING SCHOOL

I was given orders assigning me to the 73rd Transportation Heavy Boat Company, and upon my arrival in the Company, the First Sergeant asked me do I live off post. I said yes. He said,

"You can take the rest of the day off. The company commander wants to see you first thing tomorrow morning."

So, I saw the Company commander the next morning, and the first thing he said to me was Sergeant First Class Green, the Army send you here, but we do not have a diver slot here for you. I said to him that these were Army Orders, and they said that there were diver slots in the 110th Transportation Battalion. He again said that there were no diver slots here for you.

I said to him that I needed to see the Battalion Commander, and he said no problem. He made a call to the Battalion Office, and informed me he had Sergeant First

Class Green who needed to see me. Then someone in his office said bring him over. The first Sergeant, company commander and I went to the Battalion Commander Office, and he said the same thing to me that there were no slots in the Battalion for me. I said to him that I needed to see the Group commander. He said, ok.

We all went to the group commander office. He said the same thing that the others had said that there was no diver slots in the group for me. Then he said to me that I must go up to the Post Personnel Officer for further assignment. So, I went to the Post Personnel Officer. He said to me that my old MOS was surplus to the post. Someone overlooked my school status and reported my old MOS to the department of the Army Personnel office, saying that my MOS was available for any future assignment. But they failed to see that the original army orders said that the post had a vacant diver slot.

The post personnel officer said to me that I must take thirty days leave, and when I would get to my new duty assignment, I was to go to the personnel office. They would help me get my orders straightened out. I said to him, "Ok," and that was all he wanted to hear me say. So, I went back to the 73rd Transportation Heavy Boat Company. I saw the first Sergeant and told him that I need two days off. This was Friday evening, so I took two days leave, starting on Monday through Tuesday.

I went home and told my wife what happened. I then said to her that on Monday morning, we would be going to Washington, D.C., to the Pentagon to see the U. S. Army Chief Personnel Officer. We were to inquire about why my Army Orders from the Pentagon were not good at Fort Eustis, Virginia. Upon our arrival at the Pentagon, we met with the Personnel Sergeant Major. I told him about my diver assignment at Fort Eustis, Virginia. He told us to have a seat and that the Chief Personnel officer would see us soon.

The Army Personnel Officer came to the door of his office and said, "Sergeant and Mrs. Green, please come into my office". Once we were seated, he asked me, "How can I help you?" I had all of my credentials, such as my Salvage Diver badge, Certificate of Completion as a Salvage Diver and the U. S. Army orders assigning me to the 110th Transportation Battalion.

The Colonel asked my wife and me to wait a minute or two while he made two telephone calls to another section of the Pentagon. When he ended the calls, he told my wife and I, that "The U. S. Army was spending thousands of dollars annually recruiting Army Divers. He stated the reason for those expenditures was because the Army was always short of trained divers. The Colonel said, "I see that the Fort Eustis' Post Personnel Officers, the 110th Transportation Battalion and the 73rd Transportation Heavy Boat Company Commanders told you that there were no diver slots for you."

60

The Colonel said that Fort Eustis had two diving sections within the 110th Transportation Battalion, so he immediately made a telephone call to the Post Personnel Office at Fort Eustis and spoke to the Personnel Officer about an African-American diver, referring to me, who had just graduated from Army's Diving School as a Salvage Diver. He wanted to know why I was given a hard time about my diving assignment. He told the Personnel Officer that there were two diving sections within 4th Transportation Terminal Group, one diving section in the 73rd Transportation Heavy Boat Company, and the other one was in the 577th Transportation Aerial Tramway Company.

The Colonel directed the Post Personnel Officer to revoke my assignments orders which reflected my old MOS (job title) immediately. He further stated that I would have a copy of the revoked orders that day. The Colonel said to the assignments Personnel Officer "Do you understand?" The Post Personal Officer replied, "Yes, sir."

"Before he gets off duty," the Colonel said. He told the post personal that the 577th (3) Transportation Aerial Tramway Company was responsible for operating Delong Pier anchored off shore in the James River outside the channel. This Delong Pier had Aerial Tramway Cars that were used for transporting cargo from the deep-water pier area to the shore at Red Beach. This diving Section did not

61

have a Non-Commission Officer (NCO) diver qualified to oversee diving operations.

The Post Personnel Officer immediately made a telephone call to the 73rd First Sergeant and told him to send Sergeant Green up to post headquarter at once. The First Sergeant told him that Sergeant Green was on a two days pass and that he would be back on Wednesday morning. So, the Personnel Officer told the First Sergeant that it would be done as soon as I checked in on Wednesday morning.

When I checked in on Wednesday morning, the First Sergeant told me to go and see the Post Personnel Officer. He told him that he had some good news for me. He met me at his office door with his hand stretched out to my hand. He said, "Guess what, I got you off of the orders." The only reply I gave was thank you. He said, now you are being assigned to the 577th Transportation Aerial Tramway Company as a diving NCO. I reported to the 577th Transportation Aerial Tramway Company.

I immediately asked the First Sergeant where the divers assigned to my diving section were. He told me that they were working with the diving NCO in the 73rd Transportation Heavy Boat Company. I said to him that was ok, and that I would be glad to work with this diving NCO. He said to me, "No, you cannot go over there to work with him."

To my surprise, this NCO was the one who made instigation about the segregation situation regarding African-Americans in the first place by saying that my Caucasian divers were from various places in the South, such as Virginia, North Carolina, South Carolina, Georgia, Florida, Mississippi, Kentucky, Alabama, etc. He had been the one who said that these boys were not going to take orders from me.

At that time, I told the First Sergeant to have all of my divers returned to the company. This was done to get all of the company diving equipment out of the warehouse storage for inspection and to make it up for diving. The process involved checking the diving set inventory list to ensure that all items were present as per the inventory list. Such as all air hoses and telephone lines that had to be married together by using treaded twine cord and by sewing a canvas booting cover over both the air-hose and life-line telephone cable together, making each set into three hundred feet (4) length to include checking out all (4) components of the diving helmet, such as port holes, face plate gasket, spit cock valve, non-returned valve, breastplate gasket, helmet lock and pin, diver compressors and other diving equipment components.

After completing all of this work, the only thing that remained left to do was to acquire a diving barge large enough to build a house in the center of the barge. This house was to be used for storage of all the diving equipment and a place for the divers to take a break in and an area to work from. Racks had to be fabricated and welded to the barge deck to be used for hanging-up divers, air-hose and life-line on. We needed two set of racks plus setting up the diver's air compressors on metal stands welded to the deck of the barge. Cleats had to be welded on one side of the diving barge, which was used to anchor the diving ladder used to get the diver in and out of the water upon completion of each dive. We had to order a roll of two-inch diameter rope that we would cut it into various length, and to splice one end of the rope to make a large loop by back-splicing the rope together for securing the diving barge to the pier or tying it to the side of a tub boat that we would use to transport our diving barge to and from various diving sites.

Here is another area where I ran into a problem with the authority. They told me that I could not have a diving barge, because none was available in the 3rd port area. However, there were two or three flat barges visible within the 3rd port area. So, this went on back and forth between the Battalion S-4 office and my company commander and myself for about one months and a half.

In the mean-time, the senior diving NCO told the authorities that I did not have the amount of diving experience that his divers had. But when the rubber hit the road regarding deployment of a dive team, he immediately had a different tune, saying that he had some health problems that prohibited him from being deployed and all that. The S-4 officer called both of us to his office, to tell us about the emergency divers' request that was coming from the department of the Army for deployment of a dive team to Sander-Strom, Greenland.

When the 4th Transportation Terminal Group got an emergency request from the Department of the U. S. Army in Washington, D. C. requesting a diver team to assist the U. S. Coast-Guard Ship the Red Bud that was on site while serving and making repairs to a buoy at Sander-Strom Greenland. They ended up encountering an emergency situation with the anchor chain. The chain had snapped (or separated) away from a floating buoy hooked to a six-inch steel pipeline one hundred feet down under-water. This ship was on-site (frozen-in) by 12 inches of surface ice awaiting the arrival of a dive team.

Chapter 3: Military Background

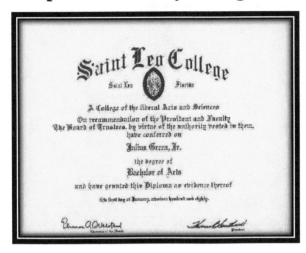

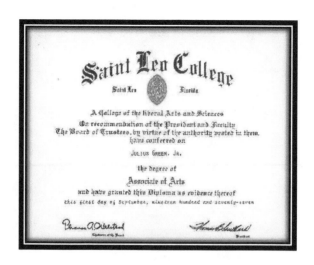

I graduated from the Transportation Non-Commission Officers (NCO) academy school with top honors in my class in 1961. I had been in the United States Army Marine Engineering class in 1967 with the rank Warrant Officer W-1. Later went on to serve on a U. S. Army vessel (ship) as a license Chief Engineer for a number of years. I attended St. Leo University and earned an Associate of Arts degree on September 01, 1977. I also earned a Bachelor of Arts degree from St. Leo University with a double major in Human Resource Administration, with a minor in Criminology on January 01, 1980.

I decided to retire from the United Army on October 1, 1973 as a Chief Warrant Officer (W-3 with twenty-two and a half years (22-½) of active-duty service). I had by then served in the U.S. Army Diving field as the Second (Black) African American for seventeen or more years, retiring with a diver rating of "Master Diver". I served as a Senior Diving Instructor with the United States Army Transportation Diving School. I attended and graduated from the Department of the U. S. Army Faculty Development Course in 1960.

Diving Assignment To Inchon Korea 1961

In 1961, I received orders for a diving assignment in Inchon, Republic of South Korea. While traveling to South Korea, I was stopped at Yokota Air Force Base in Japan to complete military processing for my South Korea assignment.

At Yokota Air Base, we were told that the Republic of South Korea was under martial law after President Syngman Rhee's Government had been overthrown by a dictator named Chung-he Park who was the President of South Korea at the time. The former President Syngman Rhee had escaped South Korea to Hawaii. As a result, South Korea had been under martial law for more than a week or less. At the end of Martial Law, we boarded a military ship and were transported to South Korea for processing at ASCOMA. Once inside the Republic of South Korea, I was issued orders for assignment with the Diving Detachment located in Inchon, South Korea, where our diving barge was located on the wall adjacent to Locks.

Inchon Port had one of the highest peak tides in the World at 35 feet between High and Low Tide. During low tide, you could walk on the mudflat for miles. You just had to be careful because when the tide returned, since that same mudflat would now be 35' feet below the water.

The Dive Team had two pontoon barges approximately forty feet long and thirty feet wide. These were floating

69

barges with two sea-mules self-propelled diesel engines on each barge mounted on their stern section The two barges were outfitted with the following equipment: three deep-sea diving outfits, three shallow-water diving outfits, nine scuba diving outfits and one high-pressure air compressor used for charging the twin diving air tanks. The other SCUBA equipment included fins, face masks, belts with weights, wet suits, and divers' watches. We also had a portable recompression two-man chamber that we used for diver's

medical treatment after being exposed for a long period of time on the bottom at various depths during any emergency. In addition, the barge was also outfitted with one thirty-ton crawler crane, four 55 CFM Air-Compressors, one rotary air compressor, two 30 KW Generators, one welding machine, one Air winch for dropping and retreating the barge anchor. We had the ability for jet piling into the ground or using water to extract piling from the ground during replacement of damaged pilings if needed.

We had a South Korean national chef, a mechanic who could repair anything, plus five South Korean national deck workers assigned to the diving barge. Our South Korean Crew was well experienced and had been assigned to assist U.S. Divers for many years. They were familiar with most of the jobs' requirements that we were responsible for in the Inchon Port Area in addition to our deep-water responsibilities. One of these responsibilities was to include six under-water 12' pipelines that were located five miles out in the deep water. The large T-5 Tanker Ships would come in and tire up to three sets of cluster piling during the discharging of petroleum products, such as Gasoline, Diesel fuel, Jet fuel, Mo-Gas, etc.

The diver's sole mission in Korea was to maintain six 12' inch underwater petroleum pipelines used to pump various types of petroleum from the large tanker ship to a large cluster of tanks within the tank farm located on the shore five or more miles inland. We had the capability to replace rupture flex-rubber 12 inch by 20-foot-long rubber hoses used to run from attached tank-ship hook-up line down to the 12" steel pipeline down underwater in one hundred and fifty feet of water.

During my stay in South Korea in 1961, I had the opportunity to witness a hurricane. It struck during the nightly hours while the tanker ship was discharging by pumping badly needed petroleum fuel product to the tank farm inland that were used in support of all United States Forces throughout South Korea. There was no warning given regarding the hurricane. Therefore, the tanker ship was ripped out of its mooring area, cutting the petroleum line and damaging all three cluster pilings that the tanker was tied to. That ship was now loose, floating in the ocean. If, the ship captain had been notified about the incoming hurricane, he would have disconnected the rubber hose line from the ship and sail out into the sea to ride out the hurricane.

Once the hurricane had passed over, the dive team went into the emergency mode, replacing all three of the damaged cluster pilings and welding a flange to the steel 12' inch pipeline. They also reconnected one hundred and fifty feet of new 12-inch rubber flex-hose flange to flange with a rubber washer between two steel flanges using steel bolts, washers and nuts. This made the line airtight to the steel 12" inch steel pipeline. The dive team had to work straight through repairing the mooring area and all six petroleum steel lines so the tanker ship could return to continue discharging badly needed fuel to the tank farm on the shore.

The dive team members went to bed with three months remaining on our twelve months tour of duty in South Korea. To wake up with a three-month emergency extension levy by the President of the United States John F. Kennedy. Therefore, we had three additional months to serve in Korea before returning to the United States.

From Fort Eustis To Sander-Strom Greenland

CW3. Julius Green, Jr
2nd Block U. S. Army
Master Diver

The Department of Army requested a diving team to travel to Sander-Storm, Greenland to go down and locate the steel pipeline and anchor chain. They were also requested to

73

make the anchor chain ready to be pulled up to the surface where it would be reattached to the surface buoy so that all incoming fuel tanker ships would use it while delivering various types of crucial fuel products to support Sander-Greenland Air-Base. These incoming ships would hoop onto the buoy, pulling up the six-inch flex-rubber hose. They would then connect it to the fuel tanker ship discharge port flange hole. That would pump (transfer) these fuel products such as jet fuel and gasoline from the ship to various tanks within the farm inland on the U.S. Air Base approximately four to five miles away from the tanker ship.

This transfer occurred during the summer months. The fuel would be stored in various tanks within the farm tanks that are needed in support of the Air Base sole mission. This mission was to launch aircraft tanker planes into the air to meet a large concentration of airplanes, flying long distance in the air to refuel these planes in the air, and get back down on the ground to wait for the next call for air refueling.

The U.S. Coast Gourd Ship was used to service all surface buoys throughout the Antarctic region water areas. The Red Bud Ship was making sure that these buoyed and ship mooring areas were all in serviceable condition to support all incoming ships that brought crucial supplies, cargo, and various types of equipment needed in support of the Air Base. One thing we experienced while at Sander-

Strom, Greenland was that the sun would shine continually for 24 hours daily from June through late October. That was followed by 24 dark hours nightly through early May annually.

From Sander-Strom Greenland to Goose Bay Labrador

Upon completion of the dive team projects at Sander-Strom, Greenland I requested to fly to Goose-Bay, Labrador for another dive project. I made the request for transportation from Sander-Strom, Greenland to Goose Bay, Labrador, and the dive team had to wait approximately thirty days before we were picked up to be transported to Goose Bay, Labrador. The dive team mission at Goose Bay, Labrador was to do an underwater search in the water areas around the dock in the port area to locate pieces of building material that dropped over-board during underloading of various cargo ships. These items were needed by a building contractor who was constructing several barracks and storage warehouses on the U.S. Air Base at Goose Bay, Labrador. Once the dive team located and removed the building material for the contractor, they were to finish clearing all underwater debris and removing the same from the water area around the port pier. This was done so that all cargo ships that needed to be tied up at the dock where various cargo, building materials, and various types of equipment, supplies and etc. could be off-loaded by the stevedores. These items were needed in support of the U. S. Air Base mission during the winter months.

The Base received most of its supplies, such as building material and other types of equipment such as the Post Exchange supplies and food items to support the total Air Base that needed off-loading during the summer months to last the Air Base through the winter months. It was known that during the winter most of the water area normally freezes over. Therefore, cargo ships cannot navigate the heavy ice water channel without the assist of the U. S. Coast Guard Ice Breaker Ship to open up the channel by breaking the ice so that ships could navigate to their destinations.

During the dive team mission at Goose Bay, Labrador, we were asked to assist the Base Explosive Ordinance Disposal (EOD) team in their mission at the Air Base. The Base EOD team was given a project to blow up an old B-52 Bomber aircraft that was making its approach for landing on the base runway. However, it missed the runway and landed in a marsh area. Due to the age of the plane, someone at the Air Base determined that it was in the best interest of the Base to cannibalize all usable parts from the plane and have the EOD team blow up the remaining plane by the use of explosive and to write off the old plane.

The dive team continued to remove all underwater debris from all around the dock area at Goose Bay, Labrador to ensure that all incoming cargo ships from having a problem during tying up ships to the dock area for off-loading various cargo by terminal service stevedore personnel.

The dive team was called on to travel to one of the Air Force relay stations (out-post) up on the pine tree line to assist in cleaning an underground well. This well was used to supply drinking water for Air Force personnel station at the outpost. This post's responsibility was to relay all information coming from various commands to other relay stations up on the pine tree line.

While the dive team was at this relay station, we had the opportunity to visit one of the Hudson Bay Stores in the Northeastern territories. They provided various types of food supplies to assist the Eskimos and Indian population with other items that they need to exist in the Antarctic Region.

Diving In Goose Bay Labrador to Fort Eustis

Upon completion of the dive team operation at Goose Bay, Labrador, we returned to our duty station at Fort Eustis, Virginia in early October 1963.

Operation Hawk-Star #1

I had the opportunity to take a dive team that participated in supporting Operation Hawk-Star #1. This operation took place at Fort Jackson, South Carolina and through the vicinity of North and South Carolina, both during June 01 through July 01, 1964. The initial testing of the 11th Air

Assaulted Division was taking place at the same time. It was forming and testing a new multi-Air-craft Assaulted Division using various types of aircrafts such as various types of helicopters and fix-wing aircrafts to include large troops and cargo carrier aircrafts in support of the 82nd Airborne Division paratrooper's and all associated equipment. The different types of vehicles included were jeeps, trucks, tanks, supplies and other related equipment included a medical unit with a field hospital and a float bridge company with rubber pontoon boats with outboard motors associated with these unit's operations.

The dive team leader received his mission and responsibility from the 11th Air-Assaulted Headquarters during various briefing sessions. One of their responsibilities was to cover all water areas, such as dams, rivers, lakes, ponds, where large consecration of aircrafts, troops and heavy equipment and flying over to rescue any troops or equipment that fell into these waters. The first thing that the senior diver team leader had to do was to established the types of support system he needed to cover these water areas.

We also had overnight cooking equipment and a cook, two-way radios for communication and food of various types. Two high-speed boats were included for transporting the dive team members and all related dive equipment and augmented with a platoon of rubber boats with outboard motors and cruise personnel to support the dive team mission.

I was given everything that I requested. Our first dive team operation took place in a Watery Dam outside of Camden, South Carolina. Watery Dam is a large body of water with a large campsite that had large rental trailers that sleep ten or more people with cooking facilities. I rented four trailers and two cabin cruise high-speed boats for the dive team operation to include refueling of all attached rubber pontoon boats daily. The dive team leader was given authorization to rent and purchase whatever he needed to support his dive team operation as long as all related support units were at the dive team operation. He needed to provide receipts for all purchase he made at the Watery Dam Mariner Store.

The first phase of the 11th Air-Assaulted Division was for thirty days to ensure that all participating units had everything needed to support the testing of multi-aircraft operations. During the first phase, all units were given the geographic areas they would be operating from during the 11th Air-assaulted operation. The dive team was given all of the locations to including dates and times where there would be a large concertation of multi-aircrafts to include airborne paratroopers with all of their equipment that would be flying over those designated water areas. The dive team was to make sure that they would be in their designated water locations on dates and times, to assist in any and all emergency rescue operation of personnel and to retrieve any equipment that fell into the water. Upon completing the first phase of Hawk-Star #1 operation, all rental equipment was cleaned and returned to Watery Dam office and high-speed rental watercrafts were cleaned, fueled up and returned to Watery Dam Marina. All charge receipts were turned in for payments. Therefore, the dive team returned to our home station Fort Eustis, Virginia during the early part of July 1964.

OPERATION HAWK-STAR # II

The Commanding General of Hawk-Star # 1 & 2 requested that my dive team be assigned to support the 2nd phase of the testing of the 11th Air-Assaulted Multi-Air-Craft Testing operations taking place at Fort Jackson, South Carolina, and including all Dams, Rivers, Lakes, ponds up to Fort Bragg, North Carolina. The duration of this operation was approbatively ninety days. Again, the dive team leader requested the same type of support system that he used for Hawk-Star # 1 and was given the same equipment, including a platoon of rubber pontoon boats with outboard motors and a personal crew to operate these boats. The first month of operation was in the same areas. The length of the flight path in each flyover zone was approximately one and a half miles wide over the water areas. We performed that same type of operation by being on-site on the designated dates and times without failure.

Next month, we started migrating upward towards Fort Bragg, North Carolina, covering the following rivers, Gable BN, Lumber River, Wateree Lake, Little Pee Dee, and Great Pee Dee Rivers, providing support service in all the rivers, lakes, and water areas where there was large consecration of multi-aircrafts flying over and dropping equipment, airborne paratroopers, and support supplies over the designated drop zones. The airborne troops would pick up what was dropped along with supplies and would rendezvous at a designated location given to them during their mission briefing. After each rendezvous, these units would load up for the next mission.

Marine Engineering Warrant Officer Training

I attended the Marine Engineering Warrant Officers School at Fort Eustis, in the Transportation School, and after graduating from the Marine Engineering Course, I was pinned as a Warrant Officer W-1. I was assigned to the 5th Transportation Company (Heavy Boat) that was slated to be deployed to South Vietnam in 1967.

Fort Eustis had the responsibility to activate the 5th Transportation Company (Heavy Boat). They had to order twelve Landing Craft utility boats from the Reserve Moat-Ball Storage and to have these Landing Crafts inspected and serviced at various little local shipyards, making them ready for deployment to South Vietnam.

The United Army made arrangements with a local Hotel in New Bern, North Carolina, for six Marine Warrant Officers to stay for the duration of the repairs to these three Landing Crafts. However, upon our arrival at the hotel to check-in, we noticed that the hotel check-in clerks were having a problem because two of the Warrant Officers were

82

African-Americans, and the hotel was segregated and only allowed Caucasians as guests. So, after the clerks had talked it over with hotel management, we, the two African American Warrant Officers, were given rooms to stay. This was Friday evening. However, come Monday morning, we were told that they had made arrangements with the local shipyard that had purchased a four-bedroom house trailer outfitted with six single beds, sheets, pillowcases, pillows, quilts, towels, wash clothes and etc. With all of the facilities needed such as washers/dryer, cooking, two bathrooms, a large lounging area, a large refrigerator, pots, pans, etc., this was just what we needed because it was adjacent to the local shipyard, and we could all cook and wash our clothes. So, we just had to go to the Marine Base at Cherry Hill, North Carolina, to the commissary to shop for whatever supplies we needed.

My team took three Landing Craft utility boats to the local shipyard in New Bern that had the responsibility of removing all onboard equipment of each boat such as engines, pumps, generators, direct drive propulsion shafts and sending them to the shipyard repair shops, where this equipment will be disassembled, and all moving parts within each engine will be inspected and measured for tolerance. The parts that do not meet the requirements for reassembly were to be replaced. All the systems of the three vessels must meet the requirements for deployment to South Vietnam.

1. Three 671 Detroit diesel engines: this required the shipyard repair mechanics to disassemble each part in each engine, inspect them and measure their tolerance level. Those parts that do not pass the tolerance test must be replaced to include new gaskets before the engine can be reassembled and returned and mounted in each Landing Craft engine room compartment.

2. Two 35 KW generators: inspect and replace all moving parts to include new gaskets etc., and the parts that do not meet the requirements, as stated in paragraph one above.

3. Three direct drive propulsion shafts along with three propeller blades: inspect and replace all moving parts as needed.

4. Two sump pumps: inspect and replace all parts as needed to ensure that all pumps are in good serviceable operating condition.

5. Check all electric circuits throughout each vessel and make the necessary repairs to ensure that all electric circuits are in good serviceable condition.

6. Remove the gasoline engine on the upper deck behind the wheelhouse on the stern of each vessel that power the outboard anchor. Send them to the shipyard repair shop to be disassembled, inspected, and measured for tolerance. Replace all moving parts with new gaskets, and any part that does not pass the tolerance test must be

replaced to ensure the engine is in good operating condition.

7. Check anchor and cable and replace any parts that appear to be worn to ensure that cable and anchor are in good operating condition.

8. Check all air-handler units onboard on each boat and replace all parts as needed to ensure that all air-handler units are in good operating condition.

9. Check sea-strainers in the well deck that is used to keep engines cool and replace all enteral parts to ensure that each vessel is in good operating condition.

10. Check all bilge pumps in the vessels' well deck, used to remove all accumulated water or liquid from the engine room floor area, to ensure that each boat is in good operating condition for deployment.

11. Check all transfer pumps used for fuel and water and related piping throughout each boat and replace any parts as needed to ensure each boat is in good operating condition ensure for deployment.

12. Check all electric winch cables and motors on each boat and replace the parts as needed to meet the requirement for deployment.

13. Check all the systems' piping fuel and water lines throughout each boat and replace pipes as needed to meet the requirement for deployment.

14. Check all the sanitation and water piping systems running to each commode, washbasins, kitchen sinks, and showers to ensure that all systems are operating and provide good clean, hygienic conditions throughout each boat. Replace any items as needed.

15. It is the responsibility of each Chief Engineer to authorize or deny repair orders requested by the shipyard mechanic on his assigned Landing Craft utility boat while it is in the local shipyard. Once all systems are checked out and released from the shipyard, it becomes the chief engineer's responsibility to keep his boat in good mechanical condition, ready for deployment or commitments.

16. All Landing Craft utility boats are put on the Marine Railway and pulled out of the water by the local shipyard to make a thorough inspection of the hull seams, including sanding the entire underwater and surface hull, removing all rust, premising with anti-rust paint, and painting the entire exterior of each vessel with deck-gray paint.

17. Check the loading ramp by inspecting the rubber gasket, hydraulic electric ramp motor to ensure that the ramp gasket and hydraulic electric motor are in good operating condition and when closed in watertight.

18. Check the entire well deck, enlisted living quarters, galley, ship head berth, all hatch covers, and doors

gaskets to ensure that when dogged down or closed, they are made watertight. Replace all rubber gaskets if needed.

19. Check the entire wheelhouse, including shifting leavers, ship wheel, lightings, ship navigation radar, ship radio, live ship tracker, vessel tracking, and live map. Remove any rust by sanding, priming with anti-rust paint, and painting the entire walls with deck-gray paint.

20. Check each Landing Craft utility boat by inspecting their Gyro-Compass that is used to assist the vessel master or captain during navigation of his boat. Replace any internal parts as needed to ensure all Gyro-Compasses are operating at peak efficiency.

21. Check the upper superstructure deck house to ensure that all equipment such as radar etc., are working at peak efficiency

My company had twelve Landing Craft utility vessels loaded on the deck of two large coal ships. Six Landing Crafts were loaded on the deck of one coal ship using a two-hundred-ton steam floating crane, and the other six were loaded onboard the other coal ship to be shipped to South Vietnam off the shore of Voong-Tar, where our company headquarters would be located.

All of my company soldiers were loaded on two large C-41 air-crafts stations at Langley Air Force Base for transportation to Tan Son Nhut International Air Force Base outside of Saigon, South Vietnam, where the 4th Transportation Terminal Headquarters was located in the port of Saigon, Vietnam. My company came under the leadership of the 11th Transportation Brattain Headquarters located in Cat Lai, South Vietnam.

First Tour Of Duty In Vietnam

1967-1968

My first tour of duty was in U.S. Army Terminal, Vung Tau/Delta, South Vietnam. It started in March 1967 with the 5th Transportation Company (Heavy Boat). Our U-Boat's primary mission was to transport various types of urgent cargo by navigating all rivers, lakes, and open waters to the following ports of Dong Tam, Can Tho, Vinh Long, Phu Quoc, Ham Tan, and the French Fort, Baria. In addition to cargo mission, the heavy boats were used for troop moves and support of tactical operations throughout South Vietnam, assisting all United States Armed Forces that was fighting the war against the North Vietnamese Forces.

The twelve Heavy Landing Craft utility boats were to transport various types of cargo to be discharged in the port of Saigon and Newport. There we would pick up another load to be discharged in the port of Dong Tan up in the Mekong Delta in support of troops fighting in the Delta Area. Some of the types of cargo we hauled were whatever the fighting troops needed, such as ammunition, various types of fuel, mogas, jp4 jet fuel, diesel, gasoline, oil, lubrication, agent orange, other types of chemicals, and demolition material, including replacement equipment such as trucks, jeeps, mobile refrigerator trucks, various types of heavy M-1 tanks, 155 field artillery equipment such as big gun howitzers, mortars, self-propelled cannons, rockets and etc. We also transported various types of mobile cranes with chassis up to ten axles similar to truck-mounted cranes, weapons, PX supplies, and various types of food items or whatever the fighting troops needed.

The U-boat carries roll-on or drive-on and drive-off. So, all we had to do was drop the anchor and head into the port landing area, let the loading boat ramp down on the beach area. If we were carrying fuel tankers, the stevedores would have the truck cab waiting for the boat to arrive, then they would back the truck cab and hook up one of the tankers to pull them all off the boat, which could carry five fuel or water tankers, once all tanks were off. There they would backload the boat and ship this cargo to other locations within South Vietnam.

We were sailing between Da Nang, Chu-lai, Qui-Nhon. Cam Ran Bay, Vung Tau/Delta, port of Saigon, with the adjacent Newport, Can Thou, Mekong Delta, Tam Che, Vinh Long Providence, Phu Quoc, Ham Tan, Chi Minh City, Dong Tam My Tho, Vong-Ro-Bay, and many other little ports in South Vietnam. We navigated the rivers within South Vietnam during the surprise Tet Offensive that began in the early morning on January 31, 1968. This was a coordinated series of North Vietnamese attacks on more than 100 hundred cities and outposts throughout South Vietnam.

The offensive attack was an attempt to foment rebellion among the South Vietnamese population and encourage the United States to scale back on its involvement in the Vietnam War. When this occurred, my company only had three months to go before the end of our tour of duty in South Vietnam. In April 1968, my company and its personnel returned to United States Fort Eustis, Virginia.

Upon my return from Vietnam, I was again assigned to the Transportation Diving School as a senior diving instructor, and I remained in this diving assignment until 1970. During the year 1970, I was given orders for a second duty assignment to South Vietnam.

Second Tour Of Duty In South Vietnam

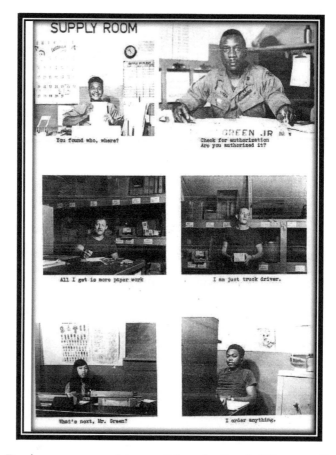

During my second tour of duty in South Vietnam, I was assigned to the 97th Transportation Company (Heavy Boat) as a supply officer in the 97th heavy boat company. The supply officer had additional responsibility for five transportation Detachments:

1. 110th Transportation Platoon (LARC-V)
2. 486th Transportation Detachment (Y-487)
3. 266th Transportation Detachment (J-Boat)

4. 271st Transportation Detachment (65] Tug Boats)

5. 567th Transportation Detachment (100'Tug)

The mission of the 97th Transportation Company (Heavy Boat) was to provide and operate landing craft for transporting personnel and heavy cargo in off-shores discharge operations and for augmenting lighterage service in a port or harbor, in inland or coastal waters, or on the open sea, including lighterage service. It is required in Joint Amphibious or other Waterborne Tactical Operations.

Active Floating Crafts: ten (10) LCUs, two (2) LCMs, one (1) J-Boat, and thirty-five (35) Barges.

110th Transportation Platoon (Watercraft) Mission: to provide tanker berthing assistance, to guard barges anchored in the stream, to support ROK elements located in areas accessible only by amphibians, and discharge cargo in the stream at Cam Ranh Bay, Phan Thiet Outpost, Phan Rang Outpost, and Nha Trang Outpost.

Active Floating Craft: fourteen (14) LARC-V's.

466th Transportation Detachment (Liquid Cargo Barge Self-Propelled) Mission: To provide crew and vessel for the transport of liquid cargo in terminals or along coastwise routes not otherwise served by MSTS.

Active Floating Craft: United States Vessel Y-487

The supply officer's responsibility is to maintain property books and inventory on all company tables of the organization (TO&E). The inventory comprises individual

92

beds, sheets and pillows, blankets, foot-lockers, and personal clothing replacements such as combat boots, socks, individual camouflage jackets, trousers, tee-shirts, underwear, individual towels, wash clothes, combat back-pact, canteens, belts, and weapons, such as 45 mm pistols, M-16 mm rifles, machine guns, trucks, jeeps trailers, large water tank, hot water heater and kitchen supplies such as refrigerators, freezers, and various food items, pots, pans, tables, chairs, etc. The supply officer must maintain separate property books for each floating detachments such as LCU'S, Tug Boats, J-Boat, M-Boats, Liquid Cargo Barge Self-Propelled, U.S. Army Vessel Y-487, and LARC-V's, with the following personnel assigned to the supply room: a supply Sergeant, a Vietnamese secretary clerk, storeroom clerk, inventory clerk, and a driver for the supply room use.

During the latter part of the Vietnam War, I was given the responsibility as Authorization Officer to deactivate the 271st transportation detachment, which had one 45'foot tub boat. I was to inventory all onboard equipment and ensure that all onboard spare parts were in good operating condition. Those that needed repair must be checked to make any repairs to ensure that all authorized equipment such as replacement parts etc. are onboard this 45' foot tug boat vessel to be transferred to the Republic of South Vietnam Armed Forces.

All I can say is that it was God grace and mercy that kept me from all harm and danger during my two tours of duty in South Vietnam as we navigated the Mekong Delta narrow rivers and other waterways during the rainy monsoon seasons in South Vietnam, where it would rain hard sometimes for an hour and other times for thirty minutes or more with the sun shining hot with a temperature of one hundred and twenty degrees.

The North Vietnamese used the monsoon season to float their explosive mines by placing the mines on a floating device in the water because the water only ran one way from July 07 through September 01, annually. They used the monsoon season to their advantage against the U.S. fighting forces, especially watercrafts navigating the rivers and other waters ways. They dropped these mines into the water, and any vessels sailing in these waters would explode when the mines would float into its hull, blowing up the ship or causing serious damage and injuring crew members.

We would request and escort PT Boat, which would be pulling a minesweeper to go in front of our U-boat, exploding any mines floating downstream during the monsoon season. We had one of our U-boat's hulls to be badly damaged by a floating mine. The floating mine could have destroyed any vessel and killed all crew members because our U-boats carried full loads of explosive cargo.

This was my last big assignment before my twelve months tour of duty ended, and I returned to the United States to be stationed at Fort Eustis, Virginia, and assigned to the Transportation School as a diving instructor.

Chapter 4: Military Medals, Awards & Achievements

➤ Awarded an Army Good Conduct Metal in 1960

➤ Awarded an Army Commendation Metal in 1960.

➤ Awarded an Army Commendation Metal (First Oak Cluster) for Meritorious Achievement in the Republic of Vietnam June 18, 1970 to September 5, 1970.

CITATION

BY DIRECTION OF THE PRESIDENT THE BRONZE STAR MEDAL

IS PRESENTED TO

CHIEF WARRANT OFFICER W2 JULIUS GREEN

UNITED STATES ARMY

For distinguishing himself by exceptionally meritorious service in connection with ground operations against a hostile force in the Republic of Vietnam during the period May 1970 to April 1971. As a result of his keen professionalism and remarkable dedication to mission fulfillment he was able to achieve maximum results in every endeavor. Each facet of his service was characterized by outstanding accomplishment and a superior manner of execution. Through his sound technical knowledge and pragmatic approach he significantly enhanced the successful accomplishment of the mission of this command. His performance was in the best traditions of the military service and reflects great credit upon himself, his unit, and the United States Army.

> ## Awarded Army Commendation Metal (Second Oak Leaf Cluster) for Meritorious Achievement in the Republic of Vietnam May 12, 1971 to October 31, 1973.

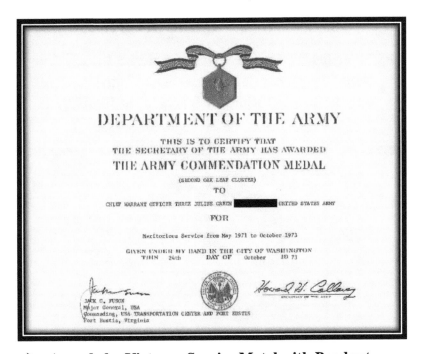

DEPARTMENT OF THE ARMY

THIS IS TO CERTIFY THAT
THE SECRETARY OF THE ARMY HAS AWARDED

THE ARMY COMMENDATION MEDAL

(SECOND OAK LEAF CLUSTER)

TO

CHIEF WARRANT OFFICER THREE JULIUS GREEN ████████ UNITED STATES ARMY

FOR

Meritorious Service from May 1971 to October 1973

GIVEN UNDER MY HAND IN THE CITY OF WASHINGTON
THIS 24th DAY OF October 19 73

JACK C. FUSON
Major General, USA
Commanding, USA TRANSPORTATION CENTER AND FORT EUSTIS
Fort Eustis, Virginia

➢ **Awarded a Vietnam Service Metal with Pendant Suspension Ribbon, with Service Ribbon in 1971.**

98

BRONZE STAR MEDAL RECIPIENT

➢ **Awarded the United States of America Bronze Star Metal for Meritorious Achievement in ground operations against hostile forces in the Republic of Vietnam in 1971.**

> **Awarded Certificate of Appreciation for Service in the U.S. Army from 1951 to 1973, signed by President Richard Nixon.**

> **Awarded in the Department of the Army: Certificate of Retirement in 1973.**

Chapter 5: Church Affiliation

At an early age, I joined the Evington Baptist Church, located out in the county on Highway Route # 3, in Allendale, South Carolina, where I maintained my membership until 1953. When I transferred to Fort Eustis, Virginia, in September 1955, I was living off base in a Pleasant Manner housing located in Hampton, Virginia. My wife and I joined Walter Temple United (Methodist) Church of Christ in Newport News, Virginia.

I served on the Trustee Board for a number of years until we received Military Family Quarters on base at Fort Eustis, Virginia. Once we moved into the Military Family Quarters, we also moved our church membership to the Base Post Chapel, where we became members, and we stayed on post until we bought a lot in Warwick Lawn. We had our home custom-built in Warwick Lawn in Denbigh, Virginia, in late 1963.

Finally, I joined Wesley United Church of Christ in early 1986, where I served on the Trustee Board for a number of years. Later, I moved up as chairman of the trustee ministry and served there for five or more years. In 2008, I was selected and trained to become a walking deacon for a period of six months, and during those six months, I met all of the requirements to receive an Ordination as a Deacon on September 31, 2008. I served in this position for a number of years and was selected by members of the deacon ministry to become Chairman of the Deacons Ministry. I served as Chairman for five or more years, and I now serve as treasurer of the deacon ministry and chairman of the church food ministry program.

A SPECIAL PART OF

HISTORYDEACON JULIUS GREEN, JR.

A Special Part of History
DEACON JULIUS GREEN

Through his entire life, Julius Green '77, '79 has defied the odds. Initially with just a 10th-grade education from a high school in Allendale, SC, Green went on to complete a successful military career, earn two college degrees, and make history along the way.

Now 81, Green joined the U.S. Army in 1951 and was stationed in Germany for three years after basic training. He then returned to Fort Jackson, SC, and decided to cross-train, as it is now known, to become a U.S. Army diver. At the time, he could not even swim, but he did not let that stop him. When he completed his training at the U.S. Army Diving School in Fort Eustis, VA, in 1956, he became only the second African American U.S. Army diver (the first graduated six months before him). Once he learned how to swim, he acquired advanced skills to become a salvage diver.

Green's challenges did not stop there. He learned that many white enlisted men from the South did not want to be led by an African American senior non-commissioned officer. So the administration at Fort Eustis quietly reassigned Green to a non-diving unit. When he heard of this, he drove two and a half hours to the Pentagon and worked his way through the bureaucratic maze. Eventually he met with an Army colonel (who happened to be from the North) who listened to his story and contacted Fort Eustis. He explained that when the Army spends thousands of dollars training a man to dive, it intends for him to do just that. He also stated that the Army does not graduate anyone from training if he is not fully prepared. Fort Eustis heard the colonel loud and clear, and Green was assigned as a training non-commissioned officer in the diving section of the 73rd Transportation Heavy Boat Company.

After 12 years as an E-6 sergeant first class, it was time for Green to be promoted to E-7 master sergeant, but all of the master sergeant spots were filled. So he applied and was accepted to the U.S. Army Marine Officers Engine Warrant Officer School. When he graduated as a warrant officer, he made history again, becoming the Army's first African American diving officer. He took on the role of instructor in the Army Diving Training Program at Fort Eustis and remained in this position until he retired in 1973. He also completed two tours in Vietnam, 1967-1968 and 1970-1971.

After he retired from the Army, Green used his leadership skills, military training, and personality to land a position as director of operations at the College of William and Mary in Williamsburg, VA. He worked there for more than 23 years and, during that time, earned an associate degree and a bachelor's degree from Saint Leo.

Today, he is proud to be part of the Saint Leo community. "Saint Leo continues to improve as it develops," Green said. "It has grown to be one of the most competitive major universities in the United States. Students need to know that they are attending an outstanding school. If Saint Leo did not exist, a lot of people would never have had the opportunity to work toward and achieve their degrees. Saint Leo made education accessible."

Julius Green has led a life that has touched so many and paved the way for others behind him. In addition to his career in the U.S. Army and at William and Mary, he is a deacon at Wesley Grove United Church of Christ in Newport News, VA. He has been a member of the Free Masons since 1956, holding local, state, and national offices and he is a life member of the Sigma Delta Chapter of Phi Beta Sigma Fraternity. He and his wife, Rosalyn, have two children, two grandchildren and three great-grandchildren.

CW3. Julius Green, Jr.
2nd Block U. S. Army
Master Diver

Chapter 6: Community And Civil Service

NAACP Local Living Legend Award – February 2005

Certification of Appreciation

Presented to

CWO Julius Green, Jr. (Ret)

The Local Living Legend Award this Day of Our Lord, February 2005 for his Significant Contributions to the Welfare and Betterment of the African- American Community and the Youth in the Tidewater Virginia Area.

By the Newport News Branch of the NAACP and the NAACP Youth Council

Charles Gray, Project Chairmen
NAACP, Newport News, VA

C.S. Florence, President
NAACP, Newport News, VA

I served as Scuba Diver Instructor, training local and State Police in Self-contained Underwater Breathing Apparatus (SCUBA) for a number of years. I served as a member of the U.S. Army Emergency Rescue Diving Team who had the responsibility of retrieving drowned victims throughout the Peninsula for a number of years. I served in various other capacities such as Past President, Vice President, and Treasurer of the United States Army Diving Association, in which all active duty and retired Army Divers work for a number of years, and I am presently a current member in good standing within the U. S. Army Association.

I am a former member of the College of William & Mary Wesley Foundation Board. I served as chairman of the board of directors for Club 33ll of Eastern Star Lodge # 13, PHA. In Hampton, Virginia, for a number of years.

Professional Organizations

I served as coordinator for Mid-Atlantic Joint Gala-Day, in which I supervised all Shrine activities relating to Gala-Day in five (5) States, North Carolina, West Virginia, Virginia, District of Columbia, and Maryland; I had the responsibility of overseeing approximately sixteen thousand (16,000) Nobles and Daughters. I am a Past Illustrious Potentate of Zem Temple # 122, Hampton, Virginia, and a Past Imperial Deputy of the Desert for Virginia in which I oversee approximately two thousand (2,000) Nobles and

106

Daughters and all Shrine Activities within Six (6) Temples in the Desert of Virginia.

- Past President of Zeta Delta Sigma Local Chapter of PHI-Beta Sigma National Fraternity.
- Former Member of Virginia Governmental Employees Association, Inc.
- Life Member of Veterans of Foreign Wars.
- Life Member of American Legion.
- Life Member of Disabled American Veterans
- Past Coordinator for Mid-Atlantic Joint Gala Day.
- Past Grand Treasurer of Prince Hall Grand Council of Royal and Select Master of Virginia.

- Graduated from the American Red Cross course on Blood Pressure Measurement and Cardiopulmonary Resuscitation on August 10, 1986.
- Graduated from the U.S. Army Pre-Commission course given at Fort Benning, Georgia, on March 24, 1961.
- Past Notary Public for the Commonwealth at large whose commission expired on January 31, 2014.

Chapter 7: Masonic And Fraternal Background

Prince Hall Affiliations:

Sovereign Grand Inspector General of the 33rd and Last Degree of Scottish Rite Freemasonry (United Supreme Council P.H.A., S.J., Grand Orient District of Columbia) * Honorary Past Imperial Potentate (Ancient Egyptian Arabic Order Nobles of the Mystic Shrine, North & South America, Inc.) * Imperial Deputy of the Desert Emeritus - Virginia * Overseer of the Work for Virginia 33rd Degree Masons * Past President Virginia Commanders of the Rite * Past Master * Past Illustrious Potentate * Past Illustrious Commander-In-Chief * Noble * Master Mason

I begin my Masonic career in 1961 at the age of 28 in Pioneer Lodge #315, located in Hampton, Virginia. The following list is a glimpse into the active memberships and various offices that I served during my masonic travels.

- ☐ Past Master of Pioneer Lodge #315 F&AM Hampton, Virginia.
- ☐ Past Commander-Chief of John W. Kirby Consistory # 40, A.A.S.R., Hampton, Virginia.
- ☐ Past Excellent High Priest, Queen of Sheba Chapter # 15, Holy Royal Arch Masons.
- ☐ Past President of Virginia Commanders of the Rites.
- ☐ Overseer of the Work for all 33° Degree Masons in the Virginia Council of Deliberation.
- ☐ Past President of Jeremiah Varner Shrine Club in 1975.
- ☐ Past Potentate of Zem Temple # 122, of A.E.A.O.N.M.S. Hampton, Virginia.
- ☐ Member of Mt. Carmel Commander # 10 Knights of Templar Newport News, Virginia.
- ☐ Member United Supreme Council 33rd Degree Masons, Southern Jurisdiction A.A.S.R. Washington, D.C
- ☐ Eastern Star Lodge # 13, PHA. 1959
- ☐ Pioneer Lodge # 315, PHA. 1961
- ☐ John W. Kirby Consistory # 40 1970
- ☐ Virginia Council of Deliberation 2008

☐ Military Vietnam Teammate given by sun Trust Bank of Nautilus 11/08/13

☐ Sister-In Law 100tth Birthday Celebration Special Plaque given by Niece and Nephews 11/27/13

☐ Looking back over the years and remembering all of the above life experiences, it shows that I have served my Country, Community, Church, and various Masonic Orders in many leadership positions with honor and integrity. Today, those characteristics and values seem to be lost.

JULIUS GREEN, JR. 33°
for
Coordinator for Mid-Atlantic
Joint Gala Day

THE DESSERT OF VIRGINIA IS SEEKING SUPPORT
FOR ITS CANDIDATE FOR COORDINATOR
FOR MID-ATLANTIC JOINT GALA DAY

Personal Data

Name:	Julius Green, Jr. 33°
Address:	25 Crutchfield Drive Newport News, Virginia 23602
Date of Birth:	January 24, 1932
Place of Birth:	Allendale, South Carolina
Marital Status:	Was married, wife deceased 2/11/83. No children.

Virginia Prince Hall Shriners Desert Conference gave its unanimous endorsement to Past Potentate Julius Green, Jr. of ZEM Temple No. 122, OASIS of Hampton, Virginia as its candidate for Coordinator of Mid-Atlantic Joint Gala Day. Past Potentate Green, was born in Allendale, South Carolina and was married to the late Lottie Cave, he is presently a member of Fort Eustis Memorial Chapter, Fort Eustis, Virginia. Past Potentate Green earned his Bachelor of Arts degree from Saint Leo College with a double major in Human Resources Administration and Criminology. He retired from the U.S. Army as a Chief Warrant Officer in Marine Engineering. After 23 years of honorable service to his country, with two tours of Vietnam.

Past Potentate Green is presently the superintendent for Support Services and Agency Fleet Manager at the College of William and Mary, located in the city of Williamsburg, Virginia.

Past Potentate Green has earned the respect of both the Nobles and Daughters through his continued dedicated service to the Prince Hall Masonic family and the community. The Virginia Desert Conference feel that through his leadership, the mid-Atlantic joint Gala Day will meet its goals and objectives in shrindon and the community.

HE HOLDS ACTIVE MEMBERSHIP IN THE FOLLOWING:

* Past Master: Eastern Star Lodge No. 13, F&A.M.; Hampton, Virginia
* Past High Priest: Queen of Sheba Chapter No. 15, Holy Royal Arch Masons
* Member: Mt. Camel Commandery No. 10, Knights Templar
* Past Commander-in-Chief: John W. Kirby Consistory No. 40, A.A.S.R.
* Past President: Club 33° Grand Inspector General's
* Past President: Jeremiah Varner Shrine Club; Newport News, Va.
* Past Potentate: Zem Temple No. 122 A.E.A.O.N.M.S., Hampton, Va.
* Member: United Supreme Council 33rd Degree Masons, Southern Jurisdiction - Class of 1975.
* Member: J. T. Maxey Bicentennial Class of '75
* Life Member & Treasurer: Phi Beta Sigma Graduate Fraternity, Inc.
* Chairman of the Board of Directors: 3311 Club, Hampton, Va.
* Life Member: Disabled American Veterans Association
* Member: Virginia Peninsula Chapter of Retired Officers Association
* Member: NAACP; Newport News, Virginia
* Member: Veterans of Foreign Wars of the United States
* American Association of Retired Persons

"Your Support is Necessary"

A Historic Diver

By Tonya S. Swindell

Sometimes history makers leave their mark quietly but strongly; such was the case with Mr. Julius Green Jr., the first black diving officer in the U.S. Army and the second African-American Master Diver for the U.S. military. With persistence, he endured challenges and persevered despite inconveniences. Mr. Green continues to impact others through his life, faith and influence.

After living in a small farming community in Allendale, S.C., Mr. Green entered the military in 1951. He served in the infantry for about five years before attending U.S. Army Diving School in Fort Eustis. As a salvage diver, he retrieved persons or items like trucks, cars and machinery on the surface or underwater.

After 12 years as a sergeant first class, Mr. Green attended U.S. Army Marine Engineering Training School. He eventually achieved the rank of Warrant Officer III. One of his responsibilities was to repair and replenish vessels before sending them to strategic locations.

One memorable assignment occurred at a shipyard within my hometown in North Carolina between 1965 and 1966. Mr. Green and three white soldiers were not allowed to reside at a hotel because of Green's race. Until completion of their 90 day assignment, the crew had to live in a four-bedroom trailer. Green also recalled being denied service at a restaurant during a recovery mission at Jamestown Ferry.

During his 22-year career, Green traveled to France, Germany and Antarctica. He served twice in Vietnam. He also went to Korea.

One rewarding mission occurred in Greenland when he located a 6-inch pipeline beneath large blocks of floating ice estimated to be about 18 inches thick. The mission continued at a Canadian Forces Base in the municipality of Happy Valley-Goose Bay, located in the province of Newfoundland and Labrador.

After the military, Mr. Green worked 23 years at the College of William & Mary until he retired as director of operations. Currently he is a Shriner, deacon and attender of a weekly breakfast club. Green is also a member of 100 Black Men of Virginia Peninsula Inc., which provides mentoring and scholarships.

Mr. Green stated, "God has been good to me." When asked about his inspiration, he described values like faith, tenacity and hard work instilled by his parents. His wife, Rosalyn, son Calvin, daughter Vivian and comrades have undoubtedly added favorable dimensions to his life also.

While serving as president of the U.S. Army Diving Association, Mr. Green interacted with Carl Brashear, the first black Master Diver for the U.S. Navy. He has been longtime friends with Tuskegee Airman Ezra Hill. And recently, Mr. Green mentioned how inspiring it was to read about Bobby Rashad Jones, a young, African-American Navy midshipman who responded jubilantly after his commencement.

Mr. Julius Green Jr. pioneered quietly and impacted our world greatly. He continually shares his influence by helping others aspire to greatness. Green presents a historic legacy as Master Diver, an officer and a gentleman.

Tonya Swindell writes a blog for www.inspirenewlife.org and is a teacher for Kingdom Building Equipping School (KBES.com). She can be reached at 1brightot@gmail.com.

Email the author

Published 10:27 pm Friday, January 11, 2019

113

- Member of J.T. Maxey Bicentennial Class of 1975, A.A.S.R.
- Past Imperial Director of Treasurer Convention Cashiers.
- Recipient of the Imperial Council (National) Legion of Honors Award.
- Past Deputy of the Desert Emeritus in December 2014.
- Honorary Past Imperial Potentate A.E.A.O.N.M.S. awarded in August 23015
- Life-Member and Treasurer Phi Beta Sigma Graduate Fraternity.
- Coronated to the Scottish Rite Grade of Sovereign Grand Inspector General in September 2015.

☐ Member of the 100 Black-Men of Virginia Peninsula Chapter Newport News, Virginia.

☐ Recognize by the Virginia Peninsula Chapter of the 100 Black-Men of America, Inc. as the **Trailblazer of the Year** during our 27th Annual Black-Tie Gala on Saturday, April 27, 2018.

☐ Recognize by the Imperial Council, as Imperial Deputy of the Oasis of Zem Temple # 122, out of 228 Temples within the Imperial Domain.

☐ Recognize by the Imperial Council, as Imperial Deputy for the Desert of Virginia, out of 48 Deserts within the Imperial Domain.

Chapter 8: Transition From U.S. Army To The College Of William & Mary

Six months prior to my retirement from the United States Army, I was allowed to seek employment from any of the local companies or institutions that had openings in my military occupation at no cost to the employer. Under this military job transition program, the U.S. Army would continue to pay my monthly salary for a period of six months, giving the potential hiring company an opportunity to observe my leadership, work ethic, initiative, enthusiasm, loyalty, character, integrity, etc.... I choose the College of William & Mary in Williamsburg, Virginia. Following my six months of military job transition, the College of William & Mary offered me an Executive Housekeeper Grade-8 position in its Department of Building and Grounds. I accepted the College of William & Mary the job opportunity and immediately submitted my request to retire from the United States Army, effective October 31, 1973.

ACADEMIC EXECUTIVE HOUSEKEEPER

During my transition, I had the opportunity to seek future employment with a number of companies and institutions; to include the likes of Hampton University, Newport News Shipyard, and finally, the College of William & Mary, where I was interviewed and hired as an Executive Housekeeper and responsible for servicing twenty or more Academic Administrative Buildings throughout the college community. There were two Executive Housekeeper positions, and the other one was located in Resident Hall and responsible for managing the care of all Students Dormitories and Housing Buildings.

Executive Housekeepers managed ninety (90) custodian employees who worked eight (8) hours daily from 5.00 A.M. to 1.00 P.M. for five and a half days. We were responsible for ensuring the weekly cleaning of all office spaces, restrooms, lounges, hallways, and stairways on three floors in each building to include policing the outside area around each building and removing all trash from offices and local areas to the trash dumpster. All Colleges and Universities throughout the United States co-sponsored and participated in the Biannual Housekeeping Seminar that was held in a designated city to enhance all Executive Housekeepers' best practices in all aspects of campus and community sanitation and cleaning to ensure the overall health and safety of students, faculty, and employees were always at the forefront of each College and University.

I attend one or more Housekeeping Seminars that taught all aspects of general cleaning, building inspections, and custodian housekeeping standards. Upon completion of the course, I was awarded an Executive Housekeepers Certificate. I remained in this position for nine (9) months only.

COLLEGE AGENCY FLEET MANAGER

The College of William & Mary had to acquire cars and various sized passenger vans from the State of Virginia, Motor Pool to be used during official travel by all College

Academic Faculty Professors, Deans, Vice Presidents, the President, including all Administrative Personnel. These vehicles were to be used for transportation in the execution of their daily duties. Authorized personnel could request a vehicle(s) from the College Agency Fleet Motor pool for a specific number of hours and/or days. The date and length of time for the use of each vehicle were required to be listed on each motor pool vehicle request form. William & Mary had approximately thirty or more vehicles in the college motor pool; and, I was responsible for ensuring that the vehicles were serviced and cleaned, and ready for pickup on the date and time requested. Upon completion trip, the vehicle would be returned to the fleet motor pool, inspected and logged in for future use. I had a transportation supervisor who took care of the agency fleet motor pool and the college bus service used for transporting students to and from various locations throughout the college community and on field trips throughout the State of Virginia and bordering states in support of various academic and sports events.

INVENTORY OF ALL COLLEGE EQUIPMENT

The Commonwealth of Virginia required all State Colleges or Universities to establish a property inventory system. This requirement came into existence because, annually, all colleges were projecting their budget requirements for the coming calendar year to include factoring in the replacement cost of various existing equipment. However, these institutions of higher learning did not have an inventory system that included the life expectancy of each piece of equipment that they were requesting State funds to replace. There was no tangible mechanism to verify the validity for requesting State and Federal Grants by Colleges and Universities.

COLLEGE INVENTORY OFFICE

I was promoted to the position of Superintendent Grade-12 for Support Services. This promotion was in line with the inventory and supply experience that I gained while serving in the military. Accurate resumes are very important for it. During one of the college's weekly briefings by the Vice President for Administration and Finance, I recall my

120

Director mentioning my military inventory and supply experience. As Superintendent, I was given an office and assumed the responsibility of establishing the inventory system for the College of William & Mary. I immediately made an assessment of what was needed to successfully make this happen. My initial list of requirements included:

(1) A Secretary

(2) Two or more Inventory Clerks

(3) Transportation to travel around campus

(4) Office furniture and equipment such as typewriters, adding machines, two-way radios, desks, office chairs, different sizes of tables, and all the other necessary things that were needed to get the system set up and running. The next thing was that my Director or the Vice President for Administration and Finance would notify all schools, college deans, department heads, and office managers, etc. This was the order of the day, and this had the college the highest priority for getting a total inventory of all college property to include all academic buildings, and student resident halls (dormitories), with no interruption by anyone in the college community. Once the property control office was set up for operation and we located where we could purchase various types of self-adhesive materials, such as listed below;

Ø Self-adhesive labels with college name and color, with numbers of six or more starting figures, like; A-123456, we ordered 20,000 to start with.

Ø Self-adhesive labels with the college name and color, with letters NSN, we ordered 20,000 to start with.

Ø Self-adhesive labels with college name and color to support Grant.

Ø Equipment funded by Federal Government Agencies to support various types of research projects that are being conducted by the college principal's investigators, with numbers six or more letters such as; G-123456, we ordered 20,000 to start with.

The property control office would select and notify a department or office about the scheduled date and time we would start his property inventory, and we would ask them to give the inventory personal their total cooperation in making this a reality. In the meantime, all colleges

were caught up in this situation, this was a priority for all institutions in establishing their annual budget, they all co-sponsored at least one property inventories conference and workshop at various locations with hotels throughout the United States, so each college of higher learning could send their Inventory Director to attend the conference and workshops that were conducted by the Society for Property

\Administrators in Washington, D. C. on December 7 & 8, '1980,

Orlando, Florida on August 24, 25, & 26 '1981 and at Massachusetts Institution of Technology (MIT) located in Boston, Massachusetts on October 18, 19 & 20 '1982, and was given a Certificate of Recognition of Successful Completion.

Society for Property Administrators

This Certificate is Presented To

JULIUS GREEN, JR.

in recognition of the successful completion
of the

Society for Property Administrators

Conference and Workshops

Orlando, FL , August 24, 25 & 26, 1981

President

Society
for
Property Administrators

This Certificate is Presented To

JULIUS GREEN, JR.

in recognition of the successful completion

of the

Society for Property Administrators

Conference and Workshops

MIT, October 18, 19 and 20, 1982

President

MOVING HAULING AND STORAGE

William & Mary College had a contract with one of its employees, who owned a number of large trucks with moving crews. This William & Mary employee was allowed to double-dip as an employee and moving contractor, as long as his moving company contract did not exceed a twenty-five thousand dollars limit. Under this agreement with the college, he supervised his moving trucks and crews. However, over the years, his contract reached the $25,000.00 limit, and the college had to terminate his moving and hauling contract.

Consequently, I was asked to assume the additional responsibility of locating two used U-Haul trucks that the college could purchase. After locating two suitable vehicles, the repair shop's Mechanical Supervisor and I performed a joint inspection and selected two (2) 35' Trucks from U-Haul's surplus inventory to be purchased by the college. Both U-Hauls were placed under the control of the college's newly established moving Office Director.

Anyone within the college community who needed to move something could make a request for movers from the moving office. I could now advertise, interview and hire crew members to continue the college's movement of equipment for offices or departments that require moving from one location to another within the college community.

My first order of business was to order the following start-up equipment;

Ø Two dozen (24) blankets to protect the movement equipment

Ø Four (4) refrigeration trucks

Ø Four (4) flatbed dolly trucks

Ø Four (4) desk mover trucks

Two hundred various sizes of heavy-duty cardboard boxes.

Ø Six (6) sets of the piano moving harness of different sizes; (2) Concert Grand Pianos, (2) Grand Pianos, and (2) Baby Grand Pianos.

Ø One dozen (12) convey rails; three sections (3) each of various sizes 6' 10' 12' and 3', six 6' curve sections, and once they are set up, you would connect them together for moving cardboard boxes.

Ø We had both U-Haul trucks checked by the college mechanics, painted with the college colors; green and gold, lettered as 'William & Mary College,' moving and hauling with college logo.

Now the college's moving and the hauling office was set up and ready to support all college moving requirements in support of all activities, such as college parties, picnics, homecoming, Charter Day, Christmas Parade, and any other events that require set up and takedown of tables, chairs, tents, etc.

FACILITY AND MAINTENANCE/OPERATIONS

Due to my military experience as a licensed Marine Engineer, who served as Chief Engineer on-board a landing craft utility vessel (ship) at Fort Eustis, Virginia, and in Vietnam, the mechanical systems in each building throughout the college community were similar. Therefore,

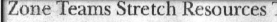

Zone Teams Stretch Resources

Plumbing, heating, air-conditioning, water pipes and underground utilities are not the kind of topics to fascinate a university audience or inspire a half-time cheer in the football stadium. The quality of life on campus, however, wouldn't be much without them all in good working order.

Paul H. Morris, director of facilities management, views these topics with more enthusiasm than most people. Since he came to campus in 1989 from the University of Colorado at Boulder, he has been guiding the College of William and Mary into the modern age of maintenance, so the rest of the campus community doesn't have to spend time worrying about leaking faucets, falling plaster or flickering lights. But, and it is a big but, says Morris, "it all takes money."

One of the first things Morris encountered on the job was a reversion of $10,800 in hourly wages and $33,500 in unrestricted funds from the 1989-90 budget and $5,500 in hourly wages and 13 full-time equivalent positions from the 1990-91 budget to the state coffers because of the downturn in the economy. Facilities management and Swem Library were the two sections of the campus that took the brunt of the reversion. "We

regrouped with the survivors and Mr. Green's skills and it has made a difference, but we are not close to providing

Paul Morris

the kind of service people on campus deserve," said Morris. "Mr. Green did not just do a good job, but an outstanding job," said Morris. Julius Green is director of operations.

Another friend of facilities manage-

127

I was selected and promoted to the position of Director of Operation, Grade-15.

o Cover Expanding Campus

Julius Green

ment during those lean year was Samuel E. Jones, associate provost for planning and budget. "Sam saved us from additional hits in '92 and actually increased our funding for the fiscal year '93 in an effort to restore funding lost to the reversions.

"Sam has always been very responsive to facilities management," adds Morris. Administrators are aware and responsive to infrastructure requirements; however, the campus continues to expand, adding more buildings, while the existing structures require just as much, if not more, of facility management's attention.

Morris is banking on passage of the $613 million bond package this fall. William and Mary hopes to get $17.1 million. Of that amount, Morris hopes $2.8 will be used for underground utility maintenance for the campus.

"If we do get the money," said Green, "it will be a tremendous help to facilities management. We need to replace worn-out infrastructures that support the academic buildings and then we have problems once we get in the buildings. Water lines, sewer lines and electricity lines break. We have to replace cables every couple of weeks. Our underground utilities are very old."

For a period now stretching into two decades, the staff of facilities management has not grown to keep pace with

the expanding campus, says Green. When the Muscarelle Museum was added, no staff was added to accommodate the added responsibility of keeping heating and cooling equipment running and properly storing art works, he points out. He also notes that no new staff was added to take care of other campus additions including the Reves Center, the faculty studio at Matoaka Lake, the Recreation Sports building, the Day Care Center, the addition to Swem Library, the reconfiguration of Blow Memorial Hall, and the law school graduate housing. The department was promised half a person for Blow, Green recalls, but that did not happen.

Morris' staff helps out with calls to residence halls, but the Office of Residence Hall Life staff has primary responsibility for maintenance in these buildings and will add to its list the new University Center, when that building is completed.

With the assistance of Director of Operations Green, Morris has set up a zone team system for academic buildings which gets the work done and gives employees a pride of ownership in their section of the campus.

Under the new zone system, a multi-maintenance team, including a plumber, electrician, heating and air conditioning specialist, one helper and a team leader, have been assigned academic buildings in a particular area of campus. Morris has also set up a quick response team which primarily handles calls about indoor/outdoor lighting on campus and night calls.

Ideally the teams would have seven members and each member would be cross-trained to fill in where necessary. Currently there are five members on each team. Morris would like to see money in his budget for cross training of team members to increase their skills and value to the team. The team leader who would be responsible for work schedules, inspections and prevention programs in his zone is also a trained specialist.

Morris would also like to see the budgeting process done with the zone system in mind. Teams and the people they serve in their zones would have input

I was responsible for managing the cross-training of each member within a team who was required to learn to perform each position or task, so all members of the team will be able to perform each task or duty in the event of sickness or vacation. This is where the college made several changes that enhanced daily productivity in the maintenance operations by establishing four (4) multi-maintenance teams and dividing all mechanical buildings, academic and resident halls into four (4) zones. One skilled mechanic was assigned to each of the four multi-maintenance teams.

Each team composition was as follows, Teams 1, 2, 3 & 4: One skilled carpenter, mechanic, electrician, plumber, and havoc.

Each of the Chief Supervisors for the above skills would perform daily inspections in each of the mechanical rooms in all buildings throughout the college community to ensure that each multi-maintenance team is performing their duties to enhance an environment that is conductive to learning for students and conformed for staff and faculty members. I was given a period of six months to implement cross-train each team and get these four multi-maintenance teams up and running.

COLLEGE POST OFFICE

A racial incident developed within the college mailroom. All the employees in the mailroom were African-Americans, except for Supervisor, who was white and had recently retired. A young, white woman who had no mailroom experience was hired as the new Supervisor over the mailroom. Despite having no experience in running a mailroom, she was hired as Supervisor, bypassing the long-time African-American employee, who was the assistant to the previous white mail room Supervisor, who had retired.

I was selected to investigate the overall situation and make my report to the Vice President for Administration and Finance. So, the Vice President for Administration and Finance had an office built within the mailroom with windows that allowed her to observe the overall mail operations from within her office. This was a disadvantage to the mailroom employees since they could not see into her office. Due to her limited knowledge in mail operation, she would call the long-time African-American assistance and pump him for information as to why the employees were not getting the work done. She was somewhat abusive to all the employees. One day, she called one of the African-American women into her office and cursed her out.

This long-time African-American lady walked out of her office into her work area and called her two sisters who were not employed by the college, she asked them to come to the mailroom, and upon their arrival, the two sisters held this young supervisor down, and they beat the devil out of her. The Vice President did not want this information to get out into the college community, so that is where I came into the picture of investigating this racial situation and making the necessary recommendations on solving the mailroom problem. I told the Vice President that those one-way windows he had installed which gave her the advantage of looking out, knowing they could not see inside. The only recommendation I made was to remove those one-way windows and replace them with regular clear glass. Since he did not want to press charges against these two ladies for trust-passing and assault on state property. This brought closure to the racial problem within the mailroom. Shortly afterward, the white lady was offered a job in the United

States Post Office in Washington, D.C. I advertised for a replacement for the newly vacant mail room Supervisor position. Eventually, I interviewed the most qualified candidates and selected the long-time African American assistant Supervisor to fill the Supervisor position.

To say the least, my selection did not make the Vice President happy. He was furious. He immediately told me to give him time to think about putting him in as Supervisor over the mailroom. I told him that this employee had lots of Assistance Supervisor experience in mail operations and procedures, and if he did not agree to hire him, there would be a real racial discrimination problem within the college community. The rest is history, he agreed with my recommendation. For a long time, the college wanted to turn the mailroom into a full U.S. Postal Office so that the government would provide the staff and faculty, and the students would be able to purchase stamps, money orders, first-class mail, etc. Everyone in the past had to travel to the City of Williamsburg Post Office, which was approximately one and a half miles away from campus and placed undue hardship on students, college staff & faculty personnel.

While I was employed at William & Mary College, I wore many hats in order to get the jobs done.

COLLEGE OF WILLIAM & MARY UNIVERSITY
ACCOLADES AND AWARDS

Ø Received numerous awards given during my twenty-two years of employment at College of William & Mary as Assistant Director of Facility and Management.

Ø The President of William & Mary College summarized Green's career by stating: dedication, professionalism, and leadership. These traits are rarely found in one individual, combined with his thorough understanding of humanity.

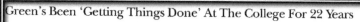

Green's Been 'Getting Things Done' At The College For 22 Years

Julius Green leaves the College after 22 years of service, most of that time spent in facilities management.

Twenty-two years after taking his first position at the College as a housekeeping supervisor, Julius Green Jr. is confident he has accomplished what he set out to do and more.

Green, director of operations in the Department of Facilities Management, retires Jan. 31.

Reflecting on his years at William and Mary, Green is proud of the current state of the College's buildings and the workers who have maintained them.

"Our buildings and infrastructure are much more efficiently maintained today than when I came here in 1973," said Green. "Facilities management employees also take much more pride in their work."

Green's success in helping to make these improvements had much to do with his determination to "get things done"— an attitude that he developed while in the army.

Facing a variety of challenges in several of the positions he has held at the College, Green said his experience in the military proved invaluable.

"I don't take 'no' for an answer when it comes to getting a job done, and I made sure all the people with whom I worked understood that," said Green.

After working in housekeeping, Green headed the property control system from 1975 to 1987. In that position, he was responsible for the development and implementation of a complete inventory of the entire College.

"Revamping property control was a massive undertaking. Yet with his organizational and leadership abilities, it was extremely successful and beneficial to the entire College community," said Paul Morris, director of facilities management.

Green began his association with the facilities aspect of the College in 1973 when it was known as the Department of Buildings and Grounds.

He assumed his current position of director of operations in 1989. Oversight

CONTINUED ON PAGE 6

CHARTERED 1693

THE COLLEGE OF WILLIAM AND MARY IN VIRGINIA
OFFICE OF THE PRESIDENT
WILLIAMSBURG, VIRGINIA 23187-8795

804 221-1693, FAX 804 221-1259

January 31, 1995

Mr. Julius Green, Jr.
Director of Operations
Facilities Management
The College of William and Mary
Williamsburg, Virginia 23185

Dear Julius:

Writing this letter causes me to feel strong emotions--sadness that such a superb colleague and remarkable leader will be leaving William and Mary, but also happiness in knowing that a new and exciting phase of life is opened before you.

It has been my privilege to have worked with you for many, many years. Our acquaintance began when I was Associate Dean of the Law School, continued when I became Dean, and now ends when I am President. When I think of the men and women with whom I have been privileged to work, I shall always remember you as an exemplar of loyalty, discipline and very top standards of performance. Those are strong memories and they will serve as an inspiration to me for as long as I am responsible for leading our College.

Both for myself and for the hundreds of others who know and respect you, I offer profound thanks for what you have done to help William and Mary and warmest wishes for happiness and good health in the future.

Most cordially,

Timothy J. Sullivan
President

134

The College of William & Mary
Interdepartmental Communication

To: Julius Green, Jr., Assistant Director, Facilities Management

From: Chairman, Commencement

Date: June 14, 1989

Subject: 1989 Commencement

    Well, as usual, it has taken far longer than it should have to express my appreciation to you for all of your help and support during Commencement weekend and in the days which preceded it. I will never stop marveling at how well you and your crews translate our requests into exactly what we had intended and need. Your job is made more complicated by the shortage of equipment, especially chairs, and yet every event came off as planned, as scheduled, and your work was done well in advance of our target periods.

    While I truly appreciate your professionalism and technical skills, I have also come to value your cooperative spirit and willingness to do whatever is required to get the job done. Having to set up the chairs in William and Mary Hall three times this year is the best example of the extent to which you are willing to go to insure that events run as intended. You shouldn't, of course, have had to do that many setups but your willingness to keep working with the arrangements until they met our needs ensured that Commencement would run as smoothly as our plans could possibly dictate.

    I hope you will pass on to all of your crews both my personal appreciation and that of the Commencement Committee for the extraordinary quality of the logistical support they provided our Commencement activities and for the wonderful way in which they contributed to the success of Commencement Weekend.

W. Samuel Sadler

WSS/tnf
cc: Paul Morris
    Roy Williams

The College Of
WILLIAM&MARY

Conference Services

P.O. Box CS
Williamsburg, VA 23187
804/221-4084

DATE: August 20, 1991

TO: Julius Green
             Facilities Management

FROM: _Bob Jeffrey, Associate Director_

             Bill Tian, Assistant Director

SUBJECT: You and Your Staff

We want to take this opportunity to thank you and your staff for providing such quality service during this past summer. From an operational standpoint, we enjoyed one of the more successful summers; and this was due in large part to the combined efforts of Facilities Management.

We especially appreciate the comments you provided on the evaluation form.

We look forward to continuing our working relationship in future summers. Please do not hesitate to call us if you have any questions or concerns.

cc: Paul Morris

/kmw

Chartered 1693

136

WILLIAM&MARY

Office of Student Affairs
W. Samuel Sadler, Vice President

Williamsburg, Virginia 23185
804/221-1236, Fax 804/221-1021

November 21, 1990

Mr. Julius Green
Superintendent for General
 Support Services
Facilities Management

Dear Mr. Green:

    I am writing to congratulate you on your newest
assignment as Director of Operations for the Department
of Facilities Management. Watching your steady
progression in responsibilities has been a real joy.
Having worked together with you throughout your tenure at
William and Mary, I know how much dedication and
professionalism you bring to your work. This latest
assignment is bound to be beneficial to the College in a
number of ways and I am delighted both for all of us and
for you at this latest acknowledgement of your skills.

    With heartiest congratulations and best wishes, I am

Sincerely,

W. Samuel Sadler
Vice President
WSS/tnf   for Student Affairs

cc: Paul Morris

Chartered 1693

Office of Student Affairs
W. Samuel Sadler, Vice President

Williamsburg, Virginia 23185
804/221-1236

May 30, 1990

Mr. Julius Green, Jr.
Assistant Director
Facilities Management

Dear Mr. Green:

In thinking about those people who deserve high praise and thanks for the successful outcome of Commencement, your name is at the top of the list. While we have come to count on your leadership and the technical support of your outstanding crew to handle the arrangements for the many events during the weekend, we assure you that your contribution is not taken for granted but rather admired and appreciated. The planning you and your staff did to make sure all of the Commencement events occurred as intended really showed this year. Furthermore, we sincerely appreciate the calm, helpful manner in which you tackle unforseen problems and new challenges.

Thank you again for all of your help with Commencement and for all of the other ways in which your presence makes William and Mary a better place. Please express our appreciation to all of those involved for their contribution of time and effort.

Sincerely,

W. Samuel Sadler

Kriss L. Fillbach

cc: Roy Williams
     Paul Morris

Chartered 1693

138

THE COLLEGE OF WILLIAM AND MARY IN VIRGINIA
MARSHALL-WYTHE SCHOOL OF LAW
OFFICE OF THE DEAN
WILLIAMSBURG, VIRGINIA 23185
804 221-3790

2 November 1990

Mr. Julius Green, Jr.
Assistant Director
Support Services
Department of Facilities Management
College of William and Mary
Williamsburg, Virginia   23185

Dear Mr. Green:

I very much appreciate your letter of 29 October in which you expressed regret for the oversight in handling arrangements for the dinner we held in honor of Chief Justice and Mrs. Rehnquist. I share your regret that we had a near disaster. I share your relief that disaster was avoided.

I do want you to know how much I value our personal and professional association over many years. I am grateful to you for the special help you have given us on many prior occasions, and I look forward to many more years of common effort for the good of William and Mary.

Most cordially,

Timothy J. Sullivan
Dean

TJS/lb
cc: W.F. Merck, II
       Dr. James Bill
       Dean Deborah Vick
       Karen Conley
       Paul H. Morris

139

DEPARTMENT OF FACILITIES MANAGEMENT

To: Julius Green, Jr.
         Assistant Director, Support Services

From: Paul H. Morris, Director
         Department of Facilities Management

Date: May 17, 1990

        I want to congratulate you and thank you and your staff for
yet another very special event executed on time and in the most
professional of manner. The ultimate compliment to anyone in
Facilities is to know that when the responsibility is delegated for
a project, that project will be done correctly and within schedule.
This, Julius, you have always done.

        The College of William and Mary and I are extremely fortunate
to have you on staff.

PHM/kft

cc: William F. Merck
     Joyce Hoar

140

THE SOCIETY OF THE ALUMNI

THE COLLEGE OF WILLIAM AND MARY

June 27, 1989

Mr. Julius Green
Superintendent Support Services
Buildings and Grounds
The College of William and Mary

Dear Mr. Green:

On behalf of the Society of the Alumni, I would like to thank you for your assistance with the logistics for our Alumni College weekend. Your help was essential to the program success and is most appreciated.

Sincerely,

Bess Littlefield
Assistant Director of Alumni Affairs

BL:eec

500 RICHMOND ROAD   POST OFFICE BOX GO
WILLIAMSBURG, VIRGINIA 23187
(804) 229-1693

141

Virginia Natural Gas

November 13, 1991

Mr. Julius Green
Director of Building & Grounds
College of William & Mary
South Boundary Street
Williamsburg, VA 23185

Dear Mr. Green:

Virginia Natural Gas, Inc. (VNG) must occasionally interrupt gas service to its interruptible customers due to gas supply and system operation considerations. Each year VNG tries to estimate the number of interruptions so that you can examine the condition of your alternate fuel system and review your supplies.

As always the number of interruptions is greatly dependent on the weather, and Hampton Roads has experienced some of the warmest winters in 40 years. If we do experience normal or colder than normal weather this winter, you should expect interruptions of up to 60 days. Please do not use the low number of interruptions in past winters as an indication of the amount of interruptions you can expect this winter.

As you know, VNG interrupted your service on November 5, 1991. This interruption was caused by a major disruption in a Columbia Gas Transmission pipeline feeding VNG. Interruptions of this nature are rare and many customers were caught by surprise. However, it did serve the purpose of reminding everyone that interruptions can occur at any time and that your alternate fuel system should be in good operating condition at all times.

VNG continually strives to minimize the number of interruptions you are subject to each year. In January 1992 VNG will complete construction of facilities that will connect the VNG distribution system to Consolidated Natural Gas Transmission. This additional interstate pipeline supply source will provide additional delivery capacity to VNG and will have a positive impact on interruptions.

If you would like to discuss this further, please call me at (804) 466-5465.

Sincerely,

Steve Baum

Steven S. Baum
Coordinator Marketing Development

142

The Institute of

Law

November 1, 1991

Julius Green, Director of Operations
Facilities Management
College of William and Mary
Williamsburg, VA 23185

Dear Mr. Green:

I am writing to express to you and your staff my
appreciation for your assistance in hosting the recent Conference
for the Federal Judiciary in Honor of the Bicentennial of the
Bill of Rights. It was the largest assemblage of federal judges
in American History--with nearly 400 federal judges in
attendance--and was a smashing success for the College. These
judges are among the most influential lawyers in America; as they
return home and spread the good word about the College, its
reputation will benefit--something that will help William and
Mary students. From all of us connected with the Institute of
Bill of Rights Law: Thank-you!

Sincerely,

Rodney A. Smolla
Arthur B. Hanson Professor of
Law and Director, Institute of
Bill of Rights Law

THE MARSHALL-WYTHE SCHOOL OF LAW • THE COLLEGE OF WILLIAM AND MARY
WILLIAMSBURG, VIRGINIA 23185 • (804) 221-3810 FAX (804) 221-3261

143

Interdepartmental Memorandum
Muscarelle Museum of Art
College of William and Mary

Date: December 10, 1991

To: Julius Green

From: Louise Kale ⨍⨍⨍

Subject:

Dear Mr. Green:

Sunday was by no means the first time John Lindsey and Jon Lawson have gone "above and beyond the call of duty" for the Museum, but it was an outstanding instance of their dedication and perseverance.

As you know, they spent a good part of Friday working on our phase I humidifier valve. John Lindsey checked with me at noon Saturday on the performance of the humidifier and determined that the boiler needed a chemical clean, which he and Jon Lawson spent most of Sunday doing. Based on the small part of this chore that I observed, it was an unpleasant and physically taxing job. They had to lower the boiler down a ladder from our mezzanine equipment room before they could even start work.

You should know that not only did they give up a large part of their weekend on our behalf, but they did so without complaint. I can only assume that they were as disappointed as the rest of us were over Ed Gillikin's reversal, but you would not have known it from their attitude, which was pleasant, positive and professional. I was impressed -- and very grateful.

I know you think highly of these two men, and I want you to know that I wholeheartedly concur with your opinion. And insofar as you know what a tight spot we are in right now, I want to thank you for your support in making the Museum a priority at this time.

cc: Paul Morris

144

The College Of
WILLIAM&MARY

Office of Student Affairs
W. Samuel Sadler, Vice President

Williamsburg, Virginia 23185
804/221-1236

May 18, 1992

Mr. Julius Green, Jr.
Assistant Director
Facilities Management

Dear Mr. Green,

We want you to know how much we appreciate the leadership and expertise you bring to the job of managing the multitude of requests and details during Commencement weekend. Your experience and understanding of what needs to be done are essential to the success of Commencement Weekend. We especially appreciate the planning and considerations which enabled you to deliver your usual level of quality service and still accommodate the addition of several major events in the weekend schedule.

Thank you and please express my appreciation to all of those involved for a job well done.

Sincerely,

W. Samuel Sadler
Chair, Commencement

Ginger M. Ambler
Assistant to the Vice President

cc: Roy Williams
      Paul Morris

Chartered 1693

145

The College Of
WILLIAM&MARY

Office of Residence Life

P.O. Box 8795
Williamsburg, VA 23187-8795
804/221-4314

MEMO

TO: Mr. Julius Green, JR., Director of Operations - Facilities Management

FROM: Chris Durden, Area Director for Ludwell & Dillard

DATE: 10/1/92

I am writing you at the request of some residents at Ludwell and Dillard who have some concern over the bus service. For the most part residents are satisfied with the buses but they do have a few problems that they wanted me to bring to your attention:

    o   residents have requested that buses run every half hour on weekends. I have explained that budget restraints make this difficult, but they wanted to request it just the same.

    o   If the buses are running early some residents have been left behind because the bus driver does not necessarily wait for residents to show up at the scheduled time.

    o   There have also been a few times this semester that students have been left behind at Dillard during shift changes. Late in the afternoon, buses will pull into the end lot at Dillard without picking up any passengers in order to switch drivers or buses. Most of the time, the new driver will swing back around to Munford and Hughes to pick up the waiting residents. Unfortunately, there have been times that the bus driver has forgotten about these people and continued onto main campus - leaving the residents to wait another half hour until it comes around again.

I appreciate your time and I hope that this feedback is helpful. Again, I would like to stress that for the most part, residents are satisfied with their bus service. Please feel free to contact me should you need clarification (221-3184).

Chartered 1693

146

William and Mary Hall

Bettie S. Adams, C.F.E.
Director

804/221-3356

P. O. Box H.C., Williamsburg, Virginia 23187

November 12, 1992

Julius Green, Jr.
Director of Operations
Facilities Management
College of William and Mary
Williamsburg, Virginia 23185

Dear Mr. Green;

For so many years we have endured a very unique
problem in the Box Office at William and Mary Hall,
that being, 85 degree temperatures during the fall
and winter months.

Many thanks to you and whomever else had a part
in correcting this problem, the Holland Heating and
Air Conditioning Company has installed a system that
more than answers our needs. We are enjoying the
capability of controlling the temperature and the unit
does a fine job of filtering the air also.

Again, I appreciate your efforts on our behalf.

Sincerely,

Bettie S. Adams
Director

BSA/fmt

cc: Paul Morris
    John Holland, Jr.

NOV 1992
Facilities
Management

Chartered 1693

147

Interdepartmental Memorandum
Muscarelle Museum of Art
College of William and Mary

Date: October 13, 1992

To: Julius Green, Jr.
           Director of Operations, Facilities Management

From: Louise Lambert Kale
           Museum Registrar

Subject: Muscarelle Museum of Art Maintenance

I am pleased and relieved to learn that the Muscarelle Museum is in line for a new humidifier boiler for phase II of the building, and I am grateful to you for your part in making this happen. I hope you have bought your last set of elements for a good long time!

I am writing now about the boiler which serves the humidifiers for phase I of the building. As you may recall, this boiler failed last fall because of massive scale build-up. John Lindsey and Jon Lawson cleaned the boiler and got it back in service. Because the performance of this boiler under the best of conditions is marginal, I am asking that it be cleaned again this fall, perhaps next month. We have been running untreated water through it for almost a year, and I am not confident that it will perform adequately throughout the coming heating season without another cleaning.

The Museum is presenting a multi-million dollar loan collection of Dutch, Flemish and German paintings as our contribution to the College's Tercentenary celebration. Many of the paintings are on wood panels, and all are extremely susceptible to fluctuations in relative humidity. For this reason, I am particularly keen to see the phase I boiler operating under optimum conditions by Christmas.

THE COLLEGE OF WILLIAM AND MARY IN VIRGINIA
OFFICE OF THE PRESIDENT
WILLIAMSBURG, VIRGINIA 23187-8795

804 221-1693, FAX 804 221-1259

October 13, 1993

Mr. Julius Green, Jr.
Director of Operations
Facilities Management
College of William and Mary

Dear Mr. Green:

Congratulations on your selection as HACE Tercentenary Employee of the
Year. It is a deserved honor, and I am proud that the selection committee
had the wisdom to make such an appropriate choice.

I look forward to hosting a luncheon in your honor at the President's
House on November 3. The occasion should provide me an opportunity
to thank you personally for all that you have done for William and Mary
over so many years.

I am honored to be on the same team with you.

Most cordially,

Timothy J. Sullivan
President

TJS:ma

149

The College Of
WILLIAM&MARY

Office of Student Affairs
W. Samuel Sadler, Vice President

Williamsburg, Virginia 23185
804/221-1236, Fax 804/221-1021

June 3, 1993

Mr. Julius Green, Jr.
Facilities Management
College of William and Mary

Dear Julius:

I cannot imagine a year with more demands on you than this one has created. Even Commencement, which should have been rather routine, proved to be more complicated than usual. In spite of our having done everything we could to mitigate any additional burden on your staff, that still happened.

But, as always, you and your crew responded in an extraordinary way. There are one or two people who are absolutely crucial to the success of a major event such as this one. You are one of those and consistently rise to the challenge and make us all look good. Your crew had to endure last minute changes, sometimes conflicting instructions, and more setups than usual and the effect must have been numbing at times. But because of your skill and the dedication of your staff, what our students and their parents and guests saw was a series of events which ran smoothly and which brought them moments of celebration and joy they will never forget.

Thank you for helping to create such a wonderful outcome and for all that you do to make William and Mary the very special place it is. You truly make a difference here.

Sincerely,

W. Samuel Sadler

WSS/tnf
cc: Vice President Merck
    Mr. Morris

Chartered 1693

150

The College Of
WILLIAM&MARY

SOCIETY OF THE ALUMNI
Office of the Executive Vice President

500 Richmond Road • P.O. Box 2100
Williamsburg, Virginia 23187-2100
804/221-1160, Fax 804/221-1186

October 26, 1993

Mr. Julius Green
25 Crutchfield Dr.
Newport News, VA 23602

Dear Julius:

Congratulations on your recent selection as HACE Tercentenary Employee of the Year. Your many contributions to the efficient and effective use of personnel and resources have been extraordinary. Through your hard work and dedication, William and Mary has become a better university and a far stronger community. Thank you for all you have done.

I look forward to the continuation of the partnership between the Society and your outstanding staff.

Warmest regards,

W. Barry Adams
Executive Vice President

WBA:egm

Charterd 1693

151

Interdepartmental Memorandum
Muscarelle Museum of Art
College of William and Mary

Date: November 11, 1993

To: Julius Green, Jr.

From: Louise Kale   *louise*

Subject: Moving Crew

I am writing to thank you for your assistance in providing a truck and crew for our trip to Norfolk last week and to tell you how indebted we are to Terry Jones, Ivey, and Wallace Poole for their good work that day. Packing and removing art from the home of a private collector requires a special effort, since we must be concerned not only with the welfare of the art, but at the same time with the goodwill of the lenders. It was a hard, tiring job, with no breaks until we were finished, but these men maintained a good attitude and professional demeanor throughout. Without them, Steve and I would <u>still</u> be in Norfolk carrying pictures down three flights of steps!

This crew is such an asset to William and Mary. Not only can we depend on them to get the job done, we can depend on them to do it well and to be pleasant while they're doing it! The Inuit drawing show opens next Friday, November 19, with a reception at the Museum from 5:30-7:00 p.m. I hope you and our "Norfolk crew" will come by to see the drawings they moved.

CERTIFICATE
of MERIT
and APPRECIATION

For exceptional performance and service during the Tercentenary year of the College of William and Mary in Virginia, this certificate acknowledges and applauds the efforts and contributions of

JULIUS GREEN, JR.

It is given with the sincere appreciation and lasting gratitude by the Society of the Alumni of the College of William and Mary.

Joseph W. Montgomery
Joseph W. Montgomery, President

Anne Nenzel Lambert
Anne Nenzel Lambert, Secretary

November 1, 1993

The College Of
WILLIAM&MARY

SOCIETY OF THE ALUMNI
Office of the Executive Vice President

500 Richmond Road • P.O. Box 2100
Williamsburg, Virginia 23187-2100
804/221-1166, Fax 804/221-1186

November 12, 1993

Julius Green, Jr.
25 Crutchfield Drive
Newport News, VA 23602

Dear Julius:

For many alumni and friends of the College of William and Mary, Homecoming 1993 marked the end of the year-long celebration of the 300th anniversary. It has been a remarkable year filled with excitement, activities and enthusiasm for the College. It has also been a year in which the campus opened its arms to thousands of additional visitors.

You have contributed to the friendliness and warmth so apparent to those who were here in 1993. Through your extraordinary commitment to job and service, the College of William and Mary was able to host the many participants and visitors in a very special way.

Your dedication is recognized as critical to the success of our programs. The enclosed Certificate of Merit and Appreciation is presented to you as a symbol of our gratitude. In addition to the certificate enclosed, a can of HUBS peanuts will be available to you from your department office as a small gift from the Society. I hope as you enjoy them you will be reminded of how much we appreciate your hard work.

Thank you.

Warmest regards,

W. Barry Adams
Executive Vice President

WBA:egm

Chartered 1693

154

Office of Student Affairs
W. Samuel Sadler, Vice President

Williamsburg, Virginia 23185
804/221-1236, Fax 804/221-1021

May 20, 1994

Julius Green
Director of Operations
Facilities Management

Dear Mr. Green:

Well, we did it again! It always amazes me when I think back on commencement weekend and realize all of the details which have to fall in place in order for us to present our graduates and their parents with. Without you and your crew, of course, none of it would be possible. I can not imagine how anyone could ask for a better working relationship or more support than you and all of your staff members provided this year. Yesterday, I had an opportunity to say that in front of the other Vice Presidents and the President. The dedication and hard work you provide day in and day out and the extraordinary results you achieve are exemplified mightily by commencement. Thank you for making this years events one of the very best ever.

Cordially,

W. Samuel Sadler
Vice President for
Student Affairs

WSS/jlm
cc: Paul Morris
     Bill Merck

Chartered 1693

155

Mr. Green
Facilities Management
College of William and Mary
Williamsburg, VA 23185

8 December 1993

Dear Mr. Green,

I am writing to thank you personally for selecting me for
the position of HVAC Technician. I value your confidence
in my experience and abilities and will work hard in my
team.

It is an honor for me to work for the College of William
and Mary. My father, Bob "Tank" Sherman was a football
coach for eight years under Coach Root in the 1970's. I
grew up on the practice fields and the side lines of the
football games. I have very fond memories of those years
that I hung around campus.

I look forward to meeting you again on January 3, 1994.
Until then, have a safe and happy holiday.

Sincerely,

Laura

Laura E. McGee

156

The College Of
WILLIAM&MARY

TO: Julius Green, Jr.

FROM: Paul H. Morris

DATE: May 16, 1994

RE: MEMORANDUM OF APPRECIATION

I want to extend my deepest thanks and appreciation for all your efforts to ensure that the '94 Commencement was successful in all areas involving Facilities Management. Though this may have been your "last commencement", all indications are that it was your "best". Your ability to coordinate the multiple logistical elements involved is to be highly commended.

Thank you, again, for all your endless efforts in support of the entire college community.

PHM/jht

xc: President Sullivan
     William F. Merck, II
     Sam Sadler

157

Williamsburg Area
CHAMBER OF COMMERCE
P.O. BOX 3620 • WILLIAMSBURG, VIRGINIA 23187-3620 • (804) 229-6511

December 16, 1994

Mr. Julius Green, Jr.
Assistant Director
Facilities Management
College of William & Mary
Williamsburg, VA 23186

Dear Mr. Green:

Thank you for your assistance with the review stand for our annual Community Christmas Parade. This event has become a special one for us all and your backing means much toward its success.

We appreciate your continued support and cooperation and look forward to next year's parade. Best wishes for a joyous holiday season!

Sincerely,

Robert W. Hershberger
Executive Vice President

RWH/pl

Serving the City of Williamsburg and the Counties of James City and York

THE BEAT GOES ON
NOVEMBER 3-6
WILLIAM G MARY
HOMECOMING '94

Memo to: Julius Green, Facilities Management

From: Sherri G. Holland '86, Director of Alumni Affairs

Date: November 28, 1994

Subject: Thank You!

You and your staff did it again! And I thank you for a job well done.

Homecoming 1994 was a tremendous success and the support of facilities management was key to that success. I know your staff worked extraordinary hours to meet many requests for set ups. They did their work beautifully and the Society is most appreciative.

Thousands of alumni left the campus with happy memories of Homecoming 1994. I hope you feel a sense of pride and satisfaction for the part you and your staff played in the success of the weekend.

William and Mary is most fortunate to have such a great team of people. Thank you!

SGH/scw

cc: Paul Morris
       Roy Williams

159

Chapter 9: How I Met My Second Wife

One night, I was home resting, and I received a telephone call from one of my fraternity brothers, who said that his wife wanted to speak with me. I said OK, and she got on the line and said to me that she had someone that she wanted me to meet and asked me if I would talk to her. I said yes, this young lady came on the line, and we talked for a while, and we exchanged telephone numbers, and I went to sleep.

You know when someone is single, look like all my fraternity brother's wives, and other organizations that I was affiliated with, and their wives who got to know me through my first wife who was a member of their Sorority Zeta Phi Beta chapter and other organizations that she held membership in, and all these folks knowing that my wife was deceased, and I was now fresh meat which would be a good fit for someone.

So, they all were busy trying to hook me up with one of their many single friends or one of their widow friends, it just did not matter to them, they just did not want to see me running loose and being a single military man with some benefit to offer. If I was the type of person who loved food and accepted all the offers that were afforded to me by various persons, some were, to my surprise - smile, I would now be an obese person. Getting on track, you know everything that looks attractive to the eyes, in some cases could be deceiving and bad for one's health. So, you know at that period that I had to be careful because in protecting my health condition due to aids, which was swiftly spreading, so I said to myself, you know that attractive young lady that you met on the phone, go back and check her out, she seems to be nice and attractive, so I followed my mine, as we got a chance to check each other out and dated for a while. I had to get the approval of one of my trusted family members, whom my first wife and I got to know and love as one true friend. Rosalyn has always been a person who showed her extraordinary intellectual ability to win friendship with mostly everyone who came in contact with her, she is a people person.

At the time we met, I had the responsibility for overseeing all Shrive Activities for Nobles and Daughters in five (5) Deserts as President of Mid-Atlantic Shrine Coalition activity in the following States, North Carolina, Virginia, West Virginia, Maryland, and the District of Columbia, and as you can see that there were lots of eligible ladies who were looking, so I needed someone to whom I could love and trust, to keep me straight and healthy. I had no children during my first marriage, and Rosalyn was divorced with a young daughter, and she had a son who needed someone to guide him. So, we got married and adopted him as our son, with her daughter's approval and the State Courts, and the rest is history. This marriage has given me lots of real love and special moments; one thing I want you - my family to know is that my first wife's family, along with all our nieces and nephews from both families, all accepted Rosalyn as their aunt once they met her. From that moment to this day, there has always been lots of love, knowing that it is her responsibility to love, honor, and take care of me. And Rosalyn has done just that over the past thirty-three (33) years without failure. So, that must have been love. And, we are looking forward to continuing this special union of love for many more years to come - with the

Lord's help and his many blessings upon us as a couple. Now, you are the judge - Smile.

Chapter 10: My Nine Vehicles

FIRST

After I joined the United States Army and served one tour of duty in Europe, I returned to the United States in December 1953 for assignment at Fort Jackson, South Carolina. I was given thirty days' leave (vacation). I went shopping for a car and was able to purchase a 1953 Chevrolet, light blue, white vinyl top, two-door coup two-door coupe. I drove that car until 1955, and then later, I gave it to my parents for their use. I then purchased a second vehicle for my use.

SECOND

Early in 1955, I purchased a 1955 Ford Crown Victory Galaxy, two-door Coupe median blue, with a white vinyl top. The car had lots of crown molding trim and white wall tires. This was a very attractive vehicle, which gave me a lot of pleasure. Everyone wanted to ride in this vehicle (smile). I kept the car until 1968.

On my first tour of duty in Vietnam, I had the opportunity to visit the post exchange (PX) located downtown in Saigon, Vietnam, where I place an order to purchase a 1968 Cadillac Coupe Deville, two doors, color turquoise with a cream Vinyl top, with lots of crown molding trim, whitewall tires. My wife and I caught a United Air Flight to downtown Detroit, Michigan Cadillac plant where everyone who had ordered a car to be made that day.

Everyone selecting their new cars, were provided a helmet with goggles and was told to follow their car chassis as it was being assembled on the assembly line. We followed our chassis as they traveled on the conveyor belt which was continuously moving.

As we followed the conveyor belt, we could see the parts coming on another belt, with parts such as front axle, rear axle, car frame body, finders, transmissions, engine, hood, wheels with tires, bumpers, etc. There were assembly-men on both sides of the car attaching these parts as the car come out, and the cars were completely assembled, each one went through the paint booth, and this booth was programmed to paint each with predetermined different colors, and at the other end of the booth there was an auto plant inspector who would run the car through an inspection line and make any adjustments as per the inspection guidelines and requirements, finally he would attach the license tags.

Everyone who picked their vehicle on that day was told to drive their cars at a certain speed engine break-in speed and not to exceed that speed for the first five hundred miles. So, the rest is history, and we got a lot of compliments on the car, as we enjoyed it.

FOURTH

In 1972, I bought a 1972 GMC Sprint Sport Coupe pick-up truck from a Buick/ Oldsmobile Dealership in Orangeburg, South Carolina. It was a two doors, tan in color, with a beige vinyl top and had lots of crown molding trim. GMC only made approximately five hundred to a thousand of those pick-up trucks each year. The GMC Sprint truck was made in competition with the Chevrolet El-Camino pickup truck. The price of this GMC Sprint Truck was $3,500.00 new when I purchased it in 1972, and I kept it for thirty or more years with over one hundred and twenty-five thousand miles on the speedometer.

However, I sold this "GMC SPRINT" for $3600.00 in 2003, after driving it for thirty or more years. At that time, it was an antique vehicle, but at the time, I had no idea, or I did not think that the vehicle was a Limited Edition and no longer was manufactured. I could have gotten a much better price for it if I had held onto it for a longer period of time. There were a lot of people inquiring about buying this truck.

FIFTH

In 1975, I purchased a Cadillac Eldorado Coupe. It was a two-door, dark maroon color with a light beige vinyl top. It also had with lots of crown molding trim and whitewall tires. The price of that new car was $7,500.00 dollars. We really did enjoy riding in an enjoyable vehicle to drive. The vehicle was heavy and it would take the road with a smooth, stable ride. I kept the vehicle until my first wife died in January 1983. We had three (3) cars at that time, so I sold the Eldorado for four thousand five hundred ($4,500.00).

SIXTH

In 1993, I purchased a new Oldsmobile Ninety-Eight, four doors sedan. It was dark blue with a dark colored vinyl top. It was fully loaded and had CB radio and a diesel engine which top of the line at that time. It was the thing to own because diesel was much cheaper than gasoline, and this was a very nice vehicle to drive. However, the dealerships did not have enough trained diesel mechanics to work on those cars during that time. After coping with various engine repairs, I converted the car from diesel to gasoline by replacing the engine and other related parts.

My brother-in-law worked for Red Devil Paint and Tools company, he was given a new car every three years (3) for private and company use, and at the completion of three years, he would get a new replacement car, He could return the car back to Red Devil, or if he had someone who wanted to buy this car at a discount price, Red Devil would honor it. So, I was able to purchase each one of these cars since the price was right. I purchased the following cars from Red Devil Tool Company over a period of time:

Ø Oldsmobile Cutlass 1983, four-door sedan

Ø Buick Rivera 1986, two-door coupe black with light black vinyl top, with black tires.

Ø Buick Rivera 2003, two-door coupe sedan light blue color overall.

Ø Chrysler 2004, LHS county town car sedan four-doors color beige with moon roof and black wall tire.

Ø Jeep Four-Wheel Drive 1998, two-doors with a dark green color. I purchased this jeep from a friend in Warwick Lawn named Bill Rhodall.

I purchased a 2003 Lincoln Navigator SUV four doors sedan beige in color with the re-traceable running board and outside mirrors; with black wall tires. This vehicle was heavy, held the road at any speed and gave you a smooth ride and was enjoyable to drive. It also accommodated seven passengers and has over a hundred and twenty thousand miles and is still runs well.

EIGHTH

I purchased a 2010 Ford Platinum Truck, new color overall bright red, a retractable moon roof, with lots of crown molding trim. It also had retractable running boards, black wall tires, and all of the extras, such as telephone, navigation system, satellite radio, telephone, with seven passengers seating. This, too, is an outstanding riding vehicle that holds the road at all speeds with a smooth ride. We have over a hundred thousand miles, and we are still enjoying it.

NINTH

We purchased a 2018 Ford Explorer Limited new SUV, seven passengers, color light gray, with four doors, satellite radio, cellular phone, negation system, retractable moon roof, with running boards, black wall tires, self-assistance parking, with outside distance motion sound system which lets you know when you are too close to an object, back-up camera.

In Conclusion Of The Story Of My Life's Journey

As this story of my life journey comes to a conclusion, everyone wants to be a part of something meaningful. Our life's record is the legacy that we leave behind, so others will remember us. Each of us is given a blank slate at the moment of our birth, and what we do with the opportunity will determine the course of our lives and the legacy that we leave behind.

We often feel a great sense of separation and loneliness when situations arise that work against our plans and dreams. Sometimes these circumstances drive a wedge between our community and us. When this happens, our immediate response should be to seek a solution that will bridge the gap and reconnect us with the familiarity of our community.

Man, by nature, has a strong desire to "BELONG" to a community. He defines his community in many ways; through physical boundaries, traditions, customs, and language. All of these variables give mankind a sense of purpose and meaning. But if we are not careful, that which defines us will absorb us. We must not allow ourselves to become discouraged by those who seem to be enjoying the temporary benefits of a life lived outside God's will.

God is faithful to deliver that what he promised to us. When you feel that you are living your life of servanthood in vain, remember that the wicked who prosper have only a temporary blessing. Perhaps your jealous spirit is just a warning that your "fuel tank" is running low, and you need to return to your source of strength, so the Lord can replenish your supply.

The Carl Brashear
Commemorative Coin

*An everlasting symbol of perseverance
and the human will to achieve greatness*

Presented to Chief Warrant Officer Three Julius Green
by the Carl Brashear Foundation

SOURCES:

Allendale County Court House 1937-1949 on the number of Schools within the County and the population of African-Americans (Black) and Caucasians (White).

All other sources of information were written from my recollection of information and memory of what has occurred during my life journey.

I would like to take this opportunity to say thanks to the following people who were very helpful and patient with me as I recounted my thoughts of events, places, dates, times, and things I observed during my lifetime. Also, the things my father did on the farm, like plowing and other tasks.

- *My wife (Rosalyn) always was kind with lots of patience who took the time to review and edit all of the written material that went into making this book of my life's journey a reality.*

- *Mrs. Debra Thompson, who assisted with spelling and some of the typing of this book. Thank you, Debra, from the bottom of my heart.*

- *Grand Inspector General Reginald A. Thompson is a Computer Technician with lots of general knowledge in all aspects of publishing and is dedicated to assisting in any way possible to get my book published.*

Thank you, Reggie.

- *Sovereign Grand Inspector General Eugene B. Coleman was always ready to drive me to where ever I needed to go or to run errands, assisting me with whatever I asked him. Thank you, Eugene.*

- *Thank you, Sovereign Grand Inspector General Albert Pierce III, who was the chief editor that arranged the events and the placement of the pictures to support all events throughout this booklet. He encouraged me to keep writing my life story and was an asset in making this book "My Life's Journey" a reality.*